Also by BRETT RUTHERFORD

Songs of the I and Thou
City Limits
The Pumpkined Heart: The Pennsylvania Poems
Anniversarius: The Book of Autumn
Doctor Jones and Other Terrors
Things Seen in Graveyards
Whippoorwill Road: The Supernatural Poems
Poems From Providence
Prometheus On Fifth Avenue
The Gods As They Are, On Their Planets
An Expectation of Presences
Trilobite Love Song
Crackers At Midnight
The Doll Without A Face

THE INHUMAN WAVE

NEW POEMS AND REVISIONS
2019-2020

by

BRETT RUTHERFORD

THE POET'S PRESS
Pittsburgh, PA

Copyright © 2020 by The Poet's Press
All Rights Reserved

Some of the poems in this book
have appeared in *Crypt of Cthulhu*, *Sensations Magazine*,
Meta-Land, and *On the Verge*,
and in the new and revised editions of
Anniversarius: The Book of Autumn,
Whippoorwill Road: The Supernatural Poems,
and *The Pumpkined Heart: Poems of Pennsylvania*.

This is the 285th publication of
THE POET'S PRESS
2209 Murray Ave #3 / Pittsburgh, PA 15217
www.poetspress.org
Contact brett@poetspress.org

Ver 1.4

CONTENTS

NEW POEMS AND REVISIONS (2019-2020)
    The Inhuman Wave   11
    Peeling the Onion   13
    Talk at the Diner   21
    The Harvest Moon in Camden   23
    Let Winter Come   26
    Two Autumn Songs   28
    The Pumpkined Heart   30
    Among the Put-Aways   32
    The Unreliable Autumn   36
    The Periodic Table: Hydrogen   38
    Letters on A Rock Outcrop   39
    The Milwaukee Intervention   40
    Squanto's Wind   51
    Son of Dracula   54
    At the Abbey of Bury St. Edmunds   59
    The Mysteries of Elsdon Churchyard   63
    Ravens Are Waiting, The Crows Have Arrived   69
    The Developer   74
    Icelandic Justice   76
    Moving to Providence, 1985   78
    Gertrude and the Revenant   81
    Domitian's Black Room   86
    I Dreamt I Was the Apennines   89
    The Old Brick House at Carpentertown   91
    The Winner   94
    The Times That Burn the Brain   95
    A Wing of Time   96
    Hither and Yon   101
    The Daemon Leads Me On   102
    1796 Edinboro Lake   103
    The Midnight Ibis   108
    March to the Scaffold   110

March au Supplice   *French version*   112
Dance of the Witches' Sabbath   114
The Cold Wave, 1958   120
Old Scholar Under Autumn Trees   128
The Man Who Hated Trees   129
The Headless Cross at Elsdon   130
The Thunderstorm (Ode 2)   133
The Mattress, Vertical   137
The Night I Almost Flew   139
They Closed His Eyes   140
He Was Not There, He Is Not Here   147
From the Lips of the Last Inca   149
Nocturne III   151
Guests at Our Country Place   154
The Secret   156
The F--- Poem   161
Being Too Much with the Stars   163
In the Mist   165
Moonlight in the Cemetery   167
The Overnight Angel   170
Becoming Invisible   171
What the Sachem's Son Told Me   172
Niagara and Back, 1966   175
Summer of 1967: Cleveland, Ohio   180
Things Done in Cities   183
After the Fugue in B Minor   184
The Agony of Orchids   185
Dead of Prose at 29   187

FATAL BIRDS OF THE SOUL
  1   Envoi   193
  2   Yet Angels Stalk   194
  3   His, The Deep Night   197
  4   What Is A Poet For?   199
  5   The Arrow Endures   200
  6   The Fate of Lovers   202
  7   The Doom of Saints   203
  8   Night of the Youthful Dead   204
  9   To Loneliness   205

10	The Inscription	208
11	The Invitation	209
12	Not of This Earth	211
13	Fatal Birds of the Soul	213
14	Spawn of the Elder Gods	215
15	The Love of the Beautiful	217
16	Some Hint of Us	219
17	Like Zephyr'd Air	220
18	The Touching Persists	221
19	The Renewing Kiss	223
20	Love and Farewell	225
21	Coda: The Undelivered Message	226

BUSTER, OR THE UNCLAIMED URN   229

ABOUT THE POEMS   247

ABOUT THE POET   260

ART CREDITS   261

ABOUT THIS BOOK   262

THE
INHUMAN
WAVE

Suffer'd much I have,
The war of men, and the inhuman wave,
Have I driven through at all parts.

    Homer, *The Odyssey*, Book 8, ll. 1614-1616.
        George Chapman translation.

THE INHUMAN WAVE

Those not Frenchmen, who found themselves
in Paris during the Terror, or in the Commune's tumult,
have told of women, the unnumbered multitude,
for every *jeune fille,* a *femme terrible,*
how they welled out of the slums and docksides
ten thousand strong with knives and hooks,
marched all the way to Versailles to rip
and shred the silk bedding of Marie Antoinette;
how with scarcely-human, distorted visages
they howled with joy as nuns and priests
were dragged to the chugging Guillotine;
how they bore the piked heads of nobles
from square to square while shriek-singing
enfants de la Patrie (enfants indeed
as the starving fishwives and worn-out
ladies of the after-hours avenged their rapes,
revenged miscarriages and hunger's stillbirths,
shook fists in the names of starved-to-death
children, of menfolk vanished to dungeons).

Those horrified witnesses to '93,
or to the doomed Commune of commons' rage,
said they had never seen such creatures,
contorted rag-faces that scarce were seen
in daylight, demons even from Goya's fever,
Maenads in '71 who hurled incendiary bombs,
Medusas of the Communards reducing the Tuileries
to an ash-ground of burnt and crumbled ruins
(damn their palaces! to the flames, their documents!) —
and how in each time of revolt, indeed,
illiterate and with no scrap of paper on them,
many a hag could issue detailed death-lists
of accumulated resentment — this way, milord,
to the alley where you will be torn to bits.
Women whose work it was to skin and scale
the Seine boats' harvest, who throttled hens,
gutted the hares and trimmed the venison —

how easily they came to blood and rending!
"Where did they all come from? One never saw
such faces! A physiognomy of anger, creatures
so hideous and filthy one could not think
they dwelt with fathers, lovers and children;
rather, they were demons of political rage,
as though every wronged, dead harridan
rose from her Black Death catacomb undead."
Mères-grand, Citoyennes, Dames de la Mort!
Beware, kings and tyrants, the women of Paris!

PEELING THE ONION

i
Summer of my fifteenth year, grandmother
spoke of the grown-up things, her secrets.
A little I knew from her mother, half-deaf
Cristina Butler, coal-stove memories
of Alsatian parents fleeing Prussians,
a grandfather who had served Napoleon
as waterboy in one of his campaigns.
The Emperor loved his men of Alsace,
those who "spoke German but sabred in French."
Things hidden in cubbyholes came down, things
my grandparents would inherit and carry on:
something in tarnished silver whose purpose
we never understood, a never-read Bible
from the Philadelphia Lutherans, and wine,
Passover wine long turned to vinegar.
There once had been a barn, long since burned down,
and you could see how far the garden had gone
when there were still men to do the tending.

But these were passed-on secrets, dimly-known.
Today grandmother Florence told me of Butler,
her father Albert, who robbed the town bank,
got thirty dollars for his trouble, caught
within hours. She showed me his photograph,
a stout man in coat and tie, Masonic pin
proudly displayed. "Dear Florence," the obverse
said in pencil-script, "The photos we took
together did not come out. Good-bye from your Pa."
"And I never saw him again," she said.
"He went to jail. No one know where he went
when he got out. Too shamed to be seen here.
I was left alone with my mother Cristina."

"But what about Homer, then?" I asked. She frowned.
Homer, the old man who had lived with Cristina
up to his death when I was eleven;
cigar-smoking recluse called "boarder" sometimes,
others said they were "secretly married."
We were told to include "Grandma Butler
and Homer" right after Grandma and Pap-Pap
in "Now I lay me down to sleep," that nightmare
prayer that threatened death by suffocation.

"Homer came later," grandmother told me.
"Nobody liked him, but he kept things safe.
We had bad years, what with the war, and then
the worst of the Depression. Nobody
had to eat except what you grew yourself."
She wiped her eyes; she was peeling onions.
Her wide peasant face, pock-marked and plain,
the face of every Alsatian village,
bent downward over her task, the skins and roots
of onions falling into the bucket
where all the waste and slops accumulate.

She held one up, pointed her knife at it.
"The truth is like this here onion." she said.
I jumped to hear her use a simile.
I leaned forward. "What do you mean, grandma?"

"See here. I peeled it So here's the white part."
She cut some more. "Now look. There's dirt again
and another layer of peel inside.
Then the rest is all white. That's just the way
some people talk to you. A lie outside,
and then a little truth, and then more lies,
until you get to the white truth inside.
I guess you've seen enough — how people are?"

Like my stepfather, I thought. My mother, too.
The double scandal of small-town affairs.
My mother, my father's sister's husband,
together now in a new town, "in sin"
as everyone called it. I lived with her
and the man I once knew as "Uncle Joe."
My father fled town when they spread the lie
that he had incest with his own sister,
gaslighting near-incest with false outrage:
they did it first, so it's all right for us.

Grandmother's house was just five miles from town.
That summer I tried to call my school-mates.
Their mothers answered the phone; each told me
their sons and daughters were just too busy,
and I shouldn't bother to call them again.
The steeple-filled streets frowned on my walking.
The place that held my ancestral tombs shunned me.

In the new town, the hated town, I said
"My parents are separated." I called
the humping couple Gertrude and Claudius.
Stepfather hated me, as I soon grew
to understand I was despised for what
I was and did, a sensitive book-worm,
hated the more for whom I resembled.

(During the courtship, if a slow dive bar
seduction can be called that, he told her
her son was a genius and ought to have
a trust fund to make sure he made his way
to some good college. A trust fund, by god!)

The false white peeled away, indeed, one day
when Uncle Joe, whiskey-drunk, said to me:
"Just so *you* know" — he never pronounced my name —
"You are not welcome here. Your father pays
child support. A bed, food on the table,
that's what you get. But when you graduate,
I want you out of here. Don't ever expect

anything from us." I later learned how
he had dumped his children from Marriage One
into an orphanage. He meant what he said.

"Grandma, I know about lies, and liars."
(I had already told her everything).
"I'm here right now to get away from them."

"Out home — this is where you can always go."
She wiped the onion tears, the anger tears.
The peels slid into the ever-swelling bucket.

ii
The house had been great-grandmother Butler's,
a four-room never-quite-finished structure,
a living-room door that never opened
since the back porch there had never been built.
It hung in air above root-cellar door.
The roof and the four walls were nothing more
than tar-paper nailed over two-by-fours.
From the road, "a shack." For Grandma, growing
from childhood to marriage, it was "Out Home."
Power it had, but no running water.
Bucket by bucket, it came from the spring,
or fell from the stormy sky into tubs,
rainfall for washing, bathing, and cooking.

I didn't mind summering there, so long
as the cache of books to read held out, so
long as there were woods to run to and from,
and the fierce night sky's Milky Way undimmed.

This morning, in the kitchen, something new:
an alarming object I had not seen
in the house or the shed or the cellar:
a shotgun (loaded?) next to the front door.
Almost on toe-tip I stood, alarmed. "What
is that?" — I pointed — "And why is it here?"

"It might be for your Uncle Joe," she answered.

I smiled at the thought. It must have belonged
to my now-dead grandfather. She saved it,
perhaps when all his things were sorted out,
the coal-miners' gear and carpenter tools
no one knew what to do with. Did she know
how to use it? What was it really for?

She said no more, but the gun stayed. Not once
was I tempted to touch or inspect it.
Its aim was at the ceiling, yes, but what
if it toppled over and shot us both?
Each night I was aware of the dark steel,
the double-barrel, the trigger so tensed
that a sleepwalker might press and fire it.

One afternoon, late, we heard someone's car
come up the long driveway, hump over the wood-
plank bridge, crack-hiss on the close-up gravel.
"Quick! Turn off the lights!" my grandma ordered.
"The TV, the radio, everything!"
She locked the door. We crouched on the carpet
beside the bed great-grandma had died in.
The shotgun lay on the quilted bedspread.
I smelled black powder and spied the brass edge
of the shotgun shells. The gun was loaded.

In the yard, I heard the chickens scatter.
A single set of heavy feet, up steps
and onto the porch. Two knocks at the door,
and then two raps on one kitchen window.
We waited. Grandma was shaking, from fear
or anger I could not be sure. She reached,
and when her hands found the shotgun she calmed.
She crouched. She was ready to aim and shoot.

At the kitchen door, an angry pounding.
"God damn it, Florence, I know you're in there!"
a bass voice shouted. "I just want to talk!"
The voice ... was the voice of my stepfather.

He pounded again, cursed. Glass did not break,
door frame did not abandon its hinges.
The steps receded. A neighbor's dog barked.
Again the chickens scattered. Another
round of curses as the rooster attacked
and chased him back to his automobile.
The engine started clumsily, gears ground
as he made the turnaround and went back
to the blacktop slope of Ore Mine Hill Road.
We waited for the normal outside sounds
to come back again: hens, robins, wind sighs
from the high pines that grazed the bedroom wall.

"What did he want?" I finally asked her. —
"He comes out here, days he's supposed to work.
He'll take me to the courthouse, he tells me.
He wants me to sign the property away
to him and your mother. He wants this house.
This is my home, your home, your mother's home,
and home to my sons when they come visit.
When Joe comes in the daytime like this, drunk
or sober, he's a bad man either way —
I just turn out the lights and I hide here.

"Drunk or insane?" I said to her. "He knows,
or ought to know, I'm here for the summer.
I guess there is no bottom to evil or stupid."

From this point on, grandma and I became
a secret alliance. Amid the slither of serpents,
she was my only friend.

iii
This time she was peeling potatoes. Peels,
eyes, and dark spots fell into the bucket.
I no longer feared the shotgun. It stood
in its place next to the kitchen door.
She looked at me, at the gun, at the knife
as it deftly pared and sliced our dinner.
"Another story I'll tell you. You're old
enough to understand it now, or you will
when the time comes to sort all the stories out.

"I was just ten when my father went to prison.
My half-sister and I were mostly off to school.
Ma was alone all day, worked herself raw to cook
and garden. She learned to can. The winter was bad.
You had to get coal for the stove, no matter what."
She pointed to the ancient coal stove, flues and pipes
set up to heat the place as well as cook and bake.

She hesitated then, and then it seemed she spoke
beyond me to someone, or in her mother's voice:
"You don't know what it's like to be a woman here
in the country, alone in the woods. Husband gone
off somewhere, or maybe dead. So a bunch of men
are sitting around in a road-house, drinking beer.
They read the paper and they see a woman's name
in the tiny print of an obituary,
or read out the address of a man sent to jail.
And, oh, they remember you. Men you hadn't seen
since you were a little girl in school. It's like they had
a list that they added to and subtracted from.

"One day a car comes down the drive. Two or three men
get out. And they take their hats off respectfully.
They have washed their hands and faces. You wouldn't think
they had jobs they should be at, and on a weekday.
They bring you a big sack of groceries. They worked hard
to think of what you might be needing, salt to flour
to cans of soup to a jar of German pickles.

They come in and sit down. They have some of your bread,
crust like none they have ever known, so they tell you.

"Somewhere in that sack there is a whiskey bottle,
so someone says, *Let's open it and have a drink!*
And you want to be polite. You get the glasses.
They have a drink. You take a drink, though it's a man's
drink and you're not accustomed to it. Then someone says
how lonely you must be without a man around.
And they laugh and make jokes until you blush.
And then they suggest something, and if you drank two
of those whiskeys and you got a little silly . . ."

She paused and looked at me. "...and you give in." Nodding,
I waited for the rest. "And if you're dumb enough
to do that, then there is no stopping it. They tell
their friends. They come by the carload to visit you.
That's the other reason I keep the shotgun here.
Because of the things that can happen to women."

iv
Grandma Florence has been dead for many years now.
Even the memory of great-grandmother Cristina grows faint.
Nothing remains of the house but its foundation.
Cousins passed by and took photographs.
They spoke to neighbors whose memories were long.
One knew all about the gang of three robbers,
how Albert Butler had gone away to prison.
They said Cristina Butler sold moonshine
right up to and past the end of Prohibition,
how cars came and went to the little "shack."

"Yes, she sold her moonshine there," the neighbor affirmed,
"but it wasn't just moonshine she sold. She sold herself
and her little daughter Florence."

The truth was in the onion, waiting.

TALK AT THE DINER

Went to the City a few weeks ago —
all clean now since those homeless folks
took off and all found jobs somewhere.
Not a speck of garbage on the street.

The beggars were gone too. One drunk
I'd always see not far from the door
of some bar or liquor store, a nod and
a wink when he'd say, "Some money
for food, for Jesus' sake." You knew
just where your quarter wound up.
Well, he's gone, and all the others,
the ones who pretended crazy or played
a scritch-scatchy violin for dollars.

Right here in town, by the tracks,
there used to be some Black folks,
but they up and moved last year.
Some factory must've given them jobs.
That Mrs. Hernandez who run the store,
the dirty one that no one would go in,
her place is all boarded up now.
They took her at night, seeing how
she had no right to be in America.

Remember those two men
who lived together, and how we'd talk,
tryin' to guess what they did at night?
They up and moved; so did those gals
we thought were kind of funny
with their short hair and all those dogs.

Used to see that bus go back and forth
talking folks in wheelchairs out
and back from the shopping mall.
Since budget cuts it doesn't run.
I wonder where those cripples went.

It takes all kinds, I say. We had ours:
that old man with the messed-up lawn
full of peace signs. That atheist poet
who'd cuss it out with the preacher
right here in the diner, and won to rights
more than half the time. Haven't seen any
of those oddballs in a long while,
but the church is getting a new steeple.

Downtown was rough at night,
least in the old days, hell, just
last year it was still bad. Bikers came,
and bad women, and men you knew
from their complexion would slit
your throat in an alley if they could.

No one in the downtown taverns now
but farmers and red-cap hunters.
A woman can walk and not worry.
Sure I see lights, and hear sirens,
but that's so late at night I don't get up
to go out and see what it is.

They're going to bulldoze a lot
of those yellow-taped houses.
Young people will move in, I'm sure.
Nice people.

Funny how all those other folks
keep moving away.
Not that I mind.

THE HARVEST MOON IN CAMDEN
(ANNIVERSARIUS XLV)

And I came, on the night of the harvest moon,
this thirteenth tropical night of the cool ninth month,
and, as I had been beckoned by bell and raven,
I found myself before a familiar tomb,
and its door was ajar and full moon showed me
the undulating form of a great serpent
(black she was and beautiful, sleek of skin
as the Queen of Sheba) and she rose up
and welcomed me. "Enter!" she said, "You
have I called, as well as many others,
and only you have tread the dream-realm,
crossed seven thresholds to stand before me.
Are you not afraid?"
                      "Afraid at *his* tomb,
he at whose knees I learned to sing and write?
Much as I fear Death, I do not fear *him*!"

And a voice inside the sepulchre uttered:
"Come, be not at all fearful. Here there is peace,
though my soul is fitful and weeping.

"I am Walt Whitman, a man, a citizen of Camden.
Reach out and touch the stone of my father,
the stone behind which my mother sleeps.
Touch this rough stone behind which my bones,
my hair, my ever-sinewed limbs, cannot slumber;
least of all my two eyes, my third eye celestial,
my mouth that cannot cease its uttering.

"For it has come to me that the land is troubled.
I ask, Has it yet come to pass that a woman sits
in the chair of Jefferson and Lincoln? I fear not,
although it is a thing much to be desired,
and it has come to me that the occupant who sits

in the White House in Washington is not a good
or a fair man; that his hands are full of gold
and not forgiveness; that a man who reads no books
attempts to make science; that corruption spreads
like black tar from a broken well across the land;

"that under poisoned air and water, the earth quakes,
fractured with the greedy extraction of gas,
that shale, which slept before the dreamings
of sauropods and tyrannosaurs, is rent
by force of water, o incompressible!
that the workmen no longer know
when their labor begins or ends, that the slaves
are not so called yet put on chains again, that men
of one color flee down the streets in terror of arms
and men of no color at all in rage pursue them;
that it is no shame among you that some are roofless
and many must bear the stain of beggary to eat;
that the sick, when they are healed, are told to pay
until their bank accounts are drained, their houses lost;
that worse than in debtors' jails the poor abide
in tents on the sidewalk, poor-towns behind
the stench-rows of oil tanks and refineries;
that the limousine-rich sell death and addiction
while mothers plead for an unpoisoned tap
from which to feed and bathe their infants,
while the Cappuccino-fueled Civil Servant says,
"Well, everyone has to die of something;"
that refugee children are caged like rabbits;
that a man with a turban or a kippa, a woman
whose faith requires a head-scarf, shall endure
the clenched fist of an ignorant mob.

"If the occupant of the White House is not
a good and fair man, or a good and fair woman,
what hope is there for the shining star
that cannot emerge from the night-cloud?

"To these states I say, as I have always said,
but even more to the people, one by one:
Resist much, and obey little.
And failing this, must the dead emerge
from their tombs to admonish you?
Have you no poets or statesmen?"

With a great sigh, the voice went dead.
I heard only a distant siren, a gunshot,
what might have been a woman's scream,
then silence. The great black snake,
which had stood erect through all the speaking,
sank to the granite floor of the tomb
and slid into the darkness. I stood,
my own shadow in solitary moonbeam
extended to the Good Gray Poet's stone
at the back of his self-made mausoleum.

LET WINTER COME
(ANNIVERSARIUS VII)

I have been here a quarter century —
now let me rest! let my contrary self
be silent this once — this year
no fancy from my leafy quill.
The lake will still eat leaves without my lines;
the unacknowledged cold drops to the bone
from dawn of equinox whether or not
some gloomy choral anthem welcomes it.

Hear me, friend: I will not send you dead trees,
the frost no longer colors me orange.

I dodge the four winds' summonings, evade
the draft of winter's war, refuse this time
to slurry down autumn with napalm frost.

Although I turn the page, my pen is dry.
Whole forms no spring can disinter
scream past me into shallow graves —
leaf-flake will go to vein and then to dust,
love that once sprung from vernal lust dies off
to tumble-leaf gravid forgetfulness.
With summer gone, the past is verdigris;
broken-off promises to peeling rust;
to the boneyard with your false embraces,
to kettle-pot sky, your terrified flight —

Leave me then; I shall be silent as frost,
sliding down autumnless to sudden snow,
ghostless too on whisper-still All Souls' Eve,
droop-walking sans pumpkins and tilted corn,
thanks-hymnless on harvest feast day, chiding
the moon to tick in slug-down count to twelfth-
month solstice and a muffled caroling.

Let winter come, if it must. I grow old
in these leaves, like an old mattress this ground
has humored me. The muffled maple-leaf
carpet accepts my tread without addressing me.

The Muse of the acorn is baffled by silence.
Ye Maple Giants, what is there to sing?
I walk by their houses; those whom I love
fold into the shadows with their lovers.
I window-watch until the blinkout freezes me.

Why do the hanging bats look down at me
that way? Why do the squirrels pause just
long enough when I see them, eye-contact
asking me why I have nothing to say?

Why, leaves, do you windlessly follow me,
clinging to my shoes and to trouser cuffs,
skittering across the bridge before me,
laughing at my failed romance, shivering
me into this my single bed and book?

Poor leaf in my pale hand, do you wonder
why in this gloom I will not write of you?
I press you to my cheek, cool, damp, and red.
You know me too well, my only friend now,
you know at the end I will not scorn to love you
though I protest my loneliness tonight.
The tree that bore you knows I will seek it,
that I will come to lean against its trunk,
waiting for dawn in the lake-edge snowing.

Bereft of leafage and loved ones, we'll watch
as lying Venus casts her pall on ice.
Why write a song that none will ever sing,
or poems that make their object
    run for the horizon?

Leave me, autumn! Silence, ye wanton winds!
Abandon, birds, these wrinkled, wretched trees!
Here are the pen, the ink, and the paper,
   the empty virgin expanse, pale yellow —
   the ruled lines pulling me down like magnets —
No! no! I have nothing at all to say —
and I will not, *will not* write a poem.

                 — *1972, New York; revised 1983, 1995, 2020*

TWO AUTUMN SONGS (ANNIVERSARIUS VI)

1

Now Autumn chills the treetops and the red flare
of my October is the herald of new deaths,
exciting yellow suicide-plummets,
ultimate green embraces, consummate
past tenses, the die-off of chlorophyll,
and as at gallows-side, the end of love.
So I join the flamboyant divers,
break with the past of my sun-sustenance,
and even with love. Forgetfulness, go!
Sleep is for summer nights. Awaken, now!

Inside my book the loved ones have grown thin.
They crumble at my touch, my tongue finds not
their lips nor the flush of their loins, but breaks
from them decay's red ash, dust on the earth,
eyeless, nameless, the walked-upon past.

2
Come that downward plummet of the world
and the stone-gray sun's last sigh,
somewhere I will be waiting at the end;
be time or age or death the house of my
endurance, I am assured of biding you.
For in the waning orbit of your life, I am
that one and only who, loving you
more than yourself, will be left by you;
   but with some gravitation
more divine than will I watch your ellipse
fade, and spend my scant affections
as the dying sun warms with his own
last fire the fleeting earth.

               — October 1969, New York; Rev. September 2019

THE PUMPKINED HEART
(ANNIVERSARIUS III)

Somewhere, the moon is red and cornstalks lean
with the wind in plucked fields. Not in New York,
city of bleached stone and desperate trees,
is my long walk of haystacks, fog in ascent,
not where traffic sings its sexless honking
can anyone mark the dim-out of frogs,
the dying-off of dragonfly wing-beats.

I am pulled up — I levitate, October-tugged,
away from the rat-doomed isle of Hudson,
clearing the water tanks and steeple-tops,
held fast on course by Orion's glimmer,
the angry scorpion tail fast behind me.
With leaves and dust I fly to my lake shore,
to the pumpkined heart, the base and the root,
the earth I touch as pole and battery.

I love this village, though it loves not me;
remember it, though it erases me.
I mark in my life, how I bear and remember
Octobers, and I know that a year is judged
by how it dies in these treetops: if it is burned
to cloud the eyes of men, or if it lies, burst
red in its full regale, waiting for snow,
     and the worms
and the spring, yes, to feed a new sun!

Earth, I am an ochre sheet of your leaves,
leaves more frequent than men in my lines,
leaves more fertile than mothers can be, leaves,
red, yellow, ambitious, how you have crept!
Leaves who have chilled my undraped lovers at night,
leaves sharing graveyard solemn caress with my lips,

leaves recurring everywhere to say their red gossip,
leaves for all I know returning again to this Fall,
   to this place, still blushing to recount
   how lovers were spent in their bed,
   leaves forever spelling the name of lost love!

You names that rise to my lips on October nights,
   you sleep-thieving echoes of aspirant heart,
   rise from the sealed tomb of years, drag shroud,
   where no leaves chatter nor branches impede
   dead, in the track of stalking remembrance — you
   who wake me alone in my grave, grave bed to recall
     each passionate urge from green twig.

Each, each and all have grown red,
   defiant in the drugged fall,
denying parentage in terrible wind,
   nonetheless breaking free,
falling to my fever in your high flame,
   red, then wet,
moist in your somber dissent, then dry, then dead,
then in my hand the brown dust
   that a seed should come to,
a leaf forever spelling the name of lost love!

                              —Revised 9/6/2019.

AMONG THE PUT-AWAYS

"Sign for your medication,
your majesty,"
the intern drones.
Lazily, I sign my usual "Z,"
which no one knows is my protest,
a toppled "N",
no use whatever
without the imperial seal
of the Bonapartes.
With a wink and a nod
he hands me the pill,
blocking the camera
as he takes it back.
Late night, in the parking lot
he will trade it for sex
with some homeless girl.

Later, the nurse comes.
"Flu shot!" she announces.
Ha! Don't I know
it's a lethal injection?
Promptly, I strangle her.
I practice Lon Chaney faces
for the cameras
until the orderlies come.

Again they want
a signature. I shake
my head "No" this time.
My friend the intern says,
"Let's double his meds,"
wink-wink, nod-nod.
And as for the nurse,
just so they will not
get in trouble, they throw
her body down
the nearest air shaft.

Out on the grounds, where
all of us exercise
amid the topiary shrubs,
I am pursued
by a hillbilly zombie,
pitchfork thrust through
his back, four tines
protruding. "I like you,"
he says, "I like you."

I do my best
at my levitation act
to avoid him. I float
just over the topiary tops
and sing in my best baritone
Over the Rainbow,
trail off after blue-birds
though no one knows anymore
what kind of thing a bird was.

Cold days, I am allowed
a corridor walk
which takes me past
the dispensary.
Renfield, the pharmacist,
shows only head to navel
at the dutch door.
"Don't worry," he cackles,
for nothing here is real."
This too, I know,
is a form of *medication,*
but I have studied hard
at epistemology,
"No!" I snap back,
"Here, *everything* is real,
in the pineal's basement."

Next day, in the shrubbery,
the undead bumpkin
comes at me again.
I know if he gets
on top of me, the blades
of the pitchfork
will go right through me
and we'd be stuck that way
forever like two bad dogs.

That was before
the men who guard us
ran off to take pot-shots
at the invading raccoons,
and just before
the howling rainstorm
that lifted the roof away
to the shouted curses
of the regional chief.

I mark this all down
since I must never forget
I was a writer,
even a trained journalist,
before all this started.
Half of the drooling mad here
were college professors.

Today the green-skinned
zombie has got rid
of his pitchfork.
I help him un-do
his coveralls. His wounds
will heal quickly
since after all,
and like the millions
of his kind out there,
he's never really going to die.

I've decided I like him, too.
He looks a bit
like Donovan,
the folk-singer,
and as for that
"eating brains" nonsense,
not to worry, he says,
he is firmly vegan.

We are planning our escape.
Whether the madhouse outside
is worse that the madhouse in,
we shall have to see.

THE UNRELIABLE AUTUMN (ANNIVERSARIUS XLVII)

It does not want to be Fall.
Not one bit of the horizon
has even a tinge of red or yellow.
The sickly sycamores, admittedly,
have gone into their crisping act,
and there's a kind of wilted edge
to random leaves at arm's reach.
Yet pole-melt and hurricane,
bird and bug absence foretell
that something awful
is out there —

the snow will come unannounced
before the pumpkin harvest.
I will awaken to its glare
that doubles the sun's intensity
on kitchen wall, draw up
the bedroom shade to see its full
white blanket wink in the parking lot,
where an acquisitive wind
will make drifts of it.

There are no clear edges any more.
No respect for solstice, equinox.
Some god of caloric anger rips skeins
off icebergs and denudes Greenlandia.
Summer goes south to pout
and meditate, while here up north,
instead of an apple- and pie-harvest,
we will shudder in all enveloping Siberia.

But nature has its seductions.
When all seems at its worst, the crocuses
line up with little flags, freezing
their delicate asses off, and you,
despite all your blizzards,
will fall for it.

With drops and heaves
and thunderings, you
will give us spring.

THE PERIODIC TABLE: HYDROGEN

You are the First One.
Once, your unity
was the Only Thing.
A hot blast of protons,
sperm stuff of the cosmos,
jostling your jillion
identical twins, up, down,
in a vibrant scream
of creative urges,
partnering in ions,
H dating H
(no law against it),

H_2 self-bonding,
converging in gas clouds,
gobbling stray neutrons,
dreaming of empire
yet eluding all,
stuff of the Ether,
the Bifrost stream
between galaxies,
ball lightning
and balloon flight,

ever at the edge
of an explosion
if oxygen is near,
holding your
secret of secrets dear:
the self-annihilating
self-fusion, the flame
at the heart of stars.
Without you, nothing;
with you, more questions
than ever answers,
light as a whisper,
    Hydrogen.

LETTERS ON A ROCK OUTCROP

Full moon shines down,
an amber glow
upon a wind-worn outcrop.

Three shapes with barely
a shadow form letters:
an "S" made up of a skull,
a torn sarape, two femurs
and some gnawed-off toes.

Inside it a smaller "S",
a same-size skull
with horn-rimmed
spectacles, a T-shirt
with a star inside a circle,
two tiny femurs,
and a blur of wind-torn
white shoelaces.

A third, and even smaller
"S" is nestled there,
and when the night chill ends,
it separates itself,
an "S" and then another
"S" until it is an undulant line
off to the horizon.
The desert snake knows where
to find the water.
Maria from Chimaltenango
did not; her son
Pablito, did not.
The moon spoke
neither K'iche nor Spanish;
the American sun
killed them.

THE MILWAUKEE INTERVENTION

A verse play-skit in one scene

Scene: Office of a shipping company. Wooden desk, old army green file cabinets, nautical maps. A window looking out over docks with a partial view of several freighters or container ships. A door backstage with glass windows, smudged.
Mrs. Caruso, early 70s, white hair in disarray, over-decorated with gaudy jewelry, wearing no nonsense work boots and a belt with a heavy key chain hanging from it. She has an old fashioned rotary phone, and a short-wave radio set with a microphone and headphones. A computer setup with an old monochrome green screen, wires and cables dangling from it.

MRS. CARUSO *(puts on headset, dials in):*
Arrigo, you there? *(Pause)* Don't "over" me, just talk.
I need to know when you get to that place,
you know, the Milwaukee location. Yeah,
just call me back when you're near. I gave you,
you know, the address and all that. Bye now.
Her daughter Irene, in a red coat, passes by the window and reaches the door. She puts her face to the glass to look inside.

IRENE
Mom, is that you in there?
Mrs Caruso takes off the headset and turns toward the door.

MRS. CARUSO
                     Who else but me?
Come on in, it's never locked, anyway.
(Who would be crazy enough to rob us?)

They hug, then Mrs. Caruso pushes her back to inspect her daughter's face.

MRS. CARUSO
You're looking better. You went to that place
I told you about? *(Irene nods)*. Good makeup helps
cover up those bruises, and all the right
vitamins will keep you in fighting form.
What's that below your eye? Show me. *Show me.*

IRENE
Nothing, mom. He —

MRS. CARUSO
             Did it again, didn't he?
Don't tell me he hit you after all that,
I mean with him in those crutches and all?

IRENE
I promised not to get you involved, mom.
I thought it was his last attempt.

MRS. CARUSO
                      Just why
would a man who got himself beaten so
he was within an inch of his life, and
had to have you feed him like a baby —
who would he go and do that?

IRENE
                 Kielbasa.

MRS. CARUSO
What the hell is *kielbasa*?

IRENE
              It's sausage,
mom, that disgusting red Polish sausage.
It's full of gristle and fat and God knows
what else, and it is so tough you just know
you're eating something the dog would refuse.
He always wants it on Friday. I gag

when I see it. I just can't cook the stuff.
So I said, *No, not this week, not ever.*

MRS. CARUSO
And so he punched you in the eye again?

IRENE
It was worse. He took the whole crutch
and swung it wide. I ducked, but it got me.
That rubber thing on the end, it just swiped
by my face and all but knocked me over.
I didn't see the black eye till later.
That was three days ago. It's almost healed.

MRS. CARUSO
I thought as much. I had my eye on him
from the morning he left the hospital.
I thought you'd be here Sunday. I worried
when you didn't call yesterday. I knew
you'd need a little more — intervention.
I don't know why you married that Pollock
bastard anyway.

IRENE
                     You liked him at first.

MRS. CARUSO
He was going to treat my daughter well,
like a princess, he said, and him being
all big and blond like that, so who was I
to doubt he would take care of you? The fool!

IRENE
It was all good until he lost his job.

MRS. CARUSO
That's what they all say. The evil they do
at the office, they do to someone else.
But watch out when they bring the troubles home!
(Looks at the short-wave radio).

Hold on, that's Arrigo. *(into mike)* Caruso here.
What's your position, Arrigo? *(to Irene).* Our barge,
the *Star of the Sea,* she's off past San Juan. *(Listens).*
Call me when you get on the satellite.
Over and out.

IRENE
                   I don't know how you manage
to keep Dad's business going.

MRS. CARUSO
                        You mean
me being a woman and all? How dare
this Italo-American widow,
the one woman who everyone expects
to spend the rest of her life in black skirts,
how dare I march in and take it over,
The Caruso Barge and Freight Line, just me,
the woman who knows nothing? On day one,
a captain came in and lifted my skirt.
He left with two fingers broken, and hell
to pay at home to explain his bruises.

IRENE
You're tough, mom. No doubt about it.

MRS. CARUSO
So then your man took off without a word?

IRENE *(surprised)*
How did you know that?

MRS. CARUSO
                     That's why you're here.

IRENE
Well, he's gone, and someone has stolen
his Harley, right from the garage. I mean,
he wasn't riding off on those crutches.
We had such a bad run with burglaries.
I didn't know what to think.

MRS. CARUSO
                          Burglaries?
Oh, you mean the gun collection? That was
a year ago, wasn't it? After he
threatened you with that AR-15?

IRENE
                                 Yes,
right after you intervened — and sent that priest.

MRS. CARUSO
Not a priest.

IRENE
                Well, he looked like a priest,
or a seminary student, all dressed
in black, and as he spoke so quietly
I couldn't make out what he said to Tad,
but I know he wound up kneeling, and made
a promise I would never be unsafe.
It was the next week we went to South Beach,
and came back and found the whole collection
was gone, cleaned out to the last bullet.

MRS. CARUSO
                                 Ha!
Just like magic. I think he sold them all,
and he was just too ashamed to tell you.

IRENE
I don't know, mom. He didn't say a word.
He never called police since half the guns
were illegal anyway.

MRS. CARUSO
                  Good riddance.
A lot of wives would like to have such luck,
to see their husband's greedy hobbies burgled.

(Phone rings)

Hold on. *(Into phone.)* Enrico, that you? What gives?
The damn Liberians won't accept it?
What's wrong with a load of fly ash and all
that damn construction waste? What do they know
about the asbestos? A dump is a dump.
(to Irene). Sorry dear, just a little business.
(into phone). Look, no one over here will take the stuff.
The Africans are too good for us, eh?
Well, there's always the nearest trench. Look on
the charts, and mind you don't spill anything.
Guess you'll just have to bring it all back home.
(Pauses). I didn't say that. You didn't hear that.

(Hangs up. Sighs). Irene, my dear, you are so innocent.
You have no idea what I do here
to keep our family and boats afloat.
So anyway, your darling Tad is gone.

IRENE
Where would he go? He can't walk?

MRS. CARUSO
                  Odds are good
he's in some dive, getting his kielbasa up
with some blond-haired lady, the kind, you know,
who do and say anything by the hour.

IRENE
Mom, no, don't be so cruel. I just want him
found. I want to know he's safe.

MRS. CARUSO
                                                    You want *what?*
Already, he had two chances. The first,
was when he hit you. *I* made him promise,
and he swore on his own mother's bones, *swore*
he would never raise his hand against you.
And then the second time, gun in your face,
the threat against you "and all your kind."
"And all your kind," let's not forget that one.
And then he hit you yet again, too drunk,
he said, to remember clearly. That's right
before he had his Harley turn over
and people he didn't see broke his legs.
You don't get a fourth chance with Carusos.

IRENE
But he is *missing*, mom! I've been calling —

MRS. CARUSO
Calling whom? It's not even three days yet —

IRENE
Emergency rooms! I just keep asking
if a man on crutches came in confused
and maybe had amnesia, you know?
I tried the police. They wouldn't listen.

MRS. CARUSO
Irene, you know how we and the police —

IRENE
I know, mom, I know. But I worry so.

MRS. CARUSO
Poor dear. Give mom a hug. You have it bad.

(They embrace. Irene cries.)

I have reason ... to believe ... that your Tad
has left you once and for all.

IRENE *(pulling away)*
                    That can't be.

MRS. CARUSO
I've had him watched. I look out for my own.
He left Sunday ... for Milwaukee.

IRENE
                    Milwaukee?
Who knows anyone in — where? — *Milwaukee?*

MRS. CARUSO
Lots of Polish folk there. He can find work.
He'll get a fake ID so no one can find him.

IRENE
But Tad is my husband. We are *married.*

MRS. CARUSO
Admit it, Irene. You came to me for help.
Just the way you would have turned to your Dad.
You know we always ... solve .... problems. That's what
family is for. You ask, and action —

IRENE *(stepping away)*
You knew he was gone ... you didn't tell me?

MRS. CARUSO
Irene, It's for the best to let him go.

(Radio call comes in.)
Hold on, Irene. ... Caruso here, over. *(Pause)*

You're in position, good? Let's just confirm:
that's nineteen — forty two — forty nine North,
sixty-seven — eighteen — thirty nine West.

(Pauses. Irene starts to walk back to the door.)

(to Irene) Don't you dare leave!
    Don't turn your back on me,
young lady. You asked for help!

IRENE
                          I *did not* ask!

MRS. CARUSO
You didn't *have* to ask in words. I saw
your face the day after he threatened you.
I saw your father's pride in those cheekbones.
(Talking into microphone).
That's it, Arrigo. Call down and tell them
to drop their cargo. Tie them together.
Any other ships in sight? Nothing — that's good.
See you guys back in Miami. Love ya'!

*(Sighs, then turns to face Irene. It is an emotional stand-off.
Each waits for the other to speak first. Irene finally bows her
head, walks over and takes a seat).*

IRENE
What am I supposed to do, mom?

MRS. CARUSO
                         Just let
the bastard go, Irene. He was rotten.

IRENE
I just can't. I *could* have done it, my way,
my time, my breaking point. But not this way,
him backing off to make me unhappy,
with nothing ever resolved.

MRS. CARUSO
                        You got no kids.
So what kind of man was that, anyway?

IRENE *(standing)*
I'll go to Milwaukee. I will find Tad.

MRS. CARUSO
You just don't see it, do you? It's all fixed.
I solved your problem. Your husband is gone.
Get on with your life. Go have some babies.
Hook up with a nice … young … Italian man.

IRENE
You will tell me where he is. Milwaukee,
where in Milwaukee?

MRS. CARUSO *(throwing up her hands)*
I am your mother. I fix it for you,
and you are ungrateful. So listen now
and learn how we do things in this real world,
this world of ships that chug the world's garbage.
There's a place out at sea, the deepest spot
you could ever go to, named for the ship
that found it: The *S.S. Milwaukee*.

Tad is in "The Milwaukee Depth." Just now
he was tied to his damn motorcycle
and dumped into the Puerto Rico Trench —

IRENE *(cries out)* Mom, *no!*

MRS. CARUSO
                Twenty … seven … thousand … feet … deep.
Squashed like a bug at the bottom, you hear?
Squashed like a bug and never to come back,
and never to hurt my little Irene!

IRENE
All along, it's been *you* behind it all,
You sent the priest who was no priest; *you* sent the burglars who took his guns, and the thugs who drove him off the road and broke his legs. What are you?

MRS. CARUSO
          My husband's wife.

IRENE
                    What am I?

MRS. CARUSO
Your father's daughter. This is how we live.

(Irene backs toward the door, looking at her mother in horror. She reaches the door, opens it from behind her without looking, and exits. She is seen running past the windows.)

MRS. CARUSO *(alone)*
(Sighs, throws up her hands).
What we do for family. No one knows.

(The phone rings.)

Caruso here. Calm seas and prosperous voyage.

(The sound of a freighter whistle.)

FINIS

SQUANTO'S WIND

A ruffian wind
content till now to move
through barricades of steel
to tug of sea,
forgetful of forest and creek,
rears up at last,
howls *No* emphatically
at the Hancock tower,
a block as gray as greed,
lunging from bedrock to sky.

The primal *No* acquires more force,
plucks glass like seeds
from a ruptured grape.

The window panes explode —
a million shards
of architectural sneeze
scattered by gravity
to punctuate the streets
with gleaming arrowheads,
obsidian spears,
black tomahawks
of dispossession.

What Manitou is this
who shakes his fist
at the barons of finance?
Whatever happened to
"Welcome, Englishmen!"
(the first words spoken
by Native to Puritan)?

The engineers move in,
revise their blueprints
while covered walkways
protect pedestrians
from Hancock's continued
defenestration.

Months pass, and yet
a lingering wind remains,
circling the sheltered walks,
lapping at plywood sheets,
a sourceless gale
that ruffles Bostonians

with its reiterated cry,
not on this land you don't.

On really windy days
the whole tower sways
and workers turn green
from motion sickness.
Millions are spent
on a counter-sliding bed
of lubricated lead
to gyro the floor to apparent
stillness; millions more
are extracted in court
from the slap-suited builders,
for fifteen hundred tons
of diagonal braces,
all to stop
the whole ziggurat
from an inevitable topple, should
just one wind, at just one angle
twist everything
into a snarl of pretzeled girders.

Finally all ten thousand panes
are, one by one, removed,
and, one by one replaced.

Is Squanto satisfied
that the tower was sold,
that the new owners slid
to bankruptcy (at least
on paper), though bankers just ooze
from one debacle to another,
awarding themselves
baronial bonuses?

No! His feathered face frowns
on clouded-over days,
to the misery of golfers;
his never-tiring gusts divert
the errant baseball, ensuring
decades of home-game dejection.
Bicyclists knocked flat
have no idea what hit them,
and every discarded lottery ticket
flies up in a miniature whirlwind
to menace dog walkers with
inexplicable paper-cuts.

It will take more than
double-dug foundations,
and wind-tunnel-tested
new window panes,
to still these vectors of rage.

Token pow-wows at shopping malls
and suburban parks
do not fool old Squanto:
sharp-dealing and inhospitable,
Boston must pay!

—Rev October 18, 2019

SON OF DRACULA
(ANNIVERSARIUS XVI)

I was the pale boy with spindly arms
    the undernourished bookworm
    dressed in baggy hand-me-downs
    (plaid shirts my father wouldn't wear,
    cut down and sewn by my mother),
old shoes in tatters, squinting all day
for need of glasses that no one would buy.

At nine, at last, they told me
    I could cross the line
to the adult part of the library
those dusty classic shelves
which no one ever seemed to touch.
I raced down the aisles,
    to G for Goethe and *Faust*
        reached up for *Frankenstein*
            at Shelley, Mary
                (not pausing at Percy Bysshe!)
            then trembled at lower S
        to find my most desired,
        most dreamt-of- —
Bram Stoker's *Dracula*.

Dracula! His doomed guest!
The vampire brides! His long, slow
spider-plot of coming to England
to drain its aristocratic blood!
His power over wolves and bats,
and a red-eyed vermin horde!
To be, himself, a bat
    or a cloud of mist,
to rest in earth
throughout the classroom day!

This was the door to years of dreams,
    and waking dreams of dreams.
I lay there nights,
the air from an open window chilling me,
waiting for the bat,
    the creeping mist,
        the leaping wolf
the caped, lean stranger.

Lulled by the lap of curtains, the false
sharp scuttle of scraping leaves,
I knew the night as the dead must know it,
waiting in caskets, dressed
in opera-house clothes
that no one living could afford to wear.

But I was not in London. Not even close.
This American river town
of blackened steeples was not my home.
Its vile taverns and shingled miseries
had no appeal to Dracula. Why would he come
when we could offer no castle,
no Carfax Abbey, no teeming streets
from which to pluck a victim?

My life — it seemed so unimportant then —
lay waiting for its sudden terminus,
its sleep and summoning to an Undead
sundown. How grand it would have been
to rise as the adopted son of Dracula!

I saw it all:
how no one would come to my grave
to see my casket covered with loam.
My mother and her loutish husband
would drink the day away at the Moose Club;
my brother would sell my books
    to buy new baseball cards;
my teachers' minds slate clean
    forgetting me, the passer-through.

(Latin I would miss,
but would Latin miss me?)

No one would hear the summoning
    as my new father called me:
Nosferatu! Arise! Arise! Nosferatu!
And I *would* rise,
    slide out of soil
        like a snake from its hollow.
He would touch my torn throat.
The wound would vanish.
He would teach me the art of flight,
the rules of the hunt
    the secret of survival.

I would not linger
    in this awful town for long.
One friend, perhaps,
    I'd make into a pale companion,
another my slave, to serve my daytime needs
(guarding my coffin,
    disposing of blood-drained bodies) —
what were friends for, anyway?

As for the rest
of this forsaken hive of humankind,
I wouldn't deign to drink its blood,
    the dregs of Europe.

We would move on
    to the cities,
to Pittsburgh first, of course,
our mist and bat-flight
unnoticed in its steel-mill choke-smoke,
the pale aristocrat and his thin son
   attending the Opera, the Symphony,
   mingling at Charity Balls,

Robin to his Batman,
   cape shadowing cape,
     fang for fang his equal soon
       at choosing whose life
         deserved abbreviation.

A fine house we'd have
   (one of several hideouts)
a private crypt below
   with the best marbles
     the finest silk, mahogany, brass
     for the coffin fittings,
our Undead mansion above
   filled to the brim with books and music...

I waited, I waited —
   He never arrived.

At thirteen, I had a night-long nosebleed,
as though my Undead half had bitten me,
drinking from within. I woke in white
of hospital bed, my veins refreshed
with the hot blood of strangers.
I had not been awake to enjoy it!
I would never even know from whom it came.

Tombstones gleamed across the hill,
lit up all night in hellish red
from the never-sleeping iron furnaces.
Leaves danced before the wardroom windows,
blew out and up to a vampire moon.

I watched it turn from copper to crimson,
    its bloating fall to tree-line,
    its deliberate feeding
   on corpuscles of oak and maple,
     one baleful eye unblinking.

A nurse brought in a tiny radio
One hour a night of symphony
was all the beauty this city could endure —
I held it close to my ear, heard Berlioz's
Fantastic Symphony: the gallows march,
the artist's Undead resurrection
amid the Witches' Sabbath —
my resurrection.

                I asked for paper.
The pen leaped forth and suddenly I knew
that I had been transformed.
I was a being of Night, I was Undead
since all around me were Unalive.

I had turned the sounds of Berlioz
and his aural Witches' Sabbath into words,
and the words, the images of night winds,
sulky witch sarabandes and wizards' orgies,
a hilltop of animal-demon-human frenzy.

The Vampire father never had to come.
I was my own father, self-made
from death's precipice.

I saw what they could not see,
walked realms of night and solitude
where law and rule and custom crumbled.
I was a poet.
I would feed on Beauty for blood,
   I would make wings of words,
      I would shun the Cross of complacency.

A cape would trail behind me always.

                — Revised and expanded October 16, 2019.

AT THE ABBEY OF BURY ST. EDMUNDS

        Had they not
        refused their fathers' blessings
        before they set out,
        masters of the league of thieves —

        Had they not
        found unguarded, thanks
        to the sextons' drunkenness,
        the Burial Church of St. Edmund —

Had they not
in eagerness for profit
pried the iron nails
from the wooden door —

Had they not
in gold-lust, that Midas curse,
tried to pry loose
the gilding
above the lintel —

Had they not
left so visible a ladder
in alleyway
as two of them clambered
up to search for gaps
in the terra-cotta —

Had they not
made noise enough
to wake the dead
with shovel, pick, and hammer
in every-which-way attack
on the portal —

Had they not
greedily indulged in
"Mushrooms, fresh today!"
at the nearby inn that night,

then off they would have gone
with the bones of St. Edmund,
some to re-sell
to ardent collectors,

some to grind up
for miracle cures,
but no! All eight
fell down in one flow
of writhing limbs, hands
clasping their tools
and implements;
down, too,
the clattering ladder.

Eyes glazed, arms frozen
in acts of desecration,
they lay inert,
till well past dawn.

The watchman found them,
paralyzed yet breathing.
The bailiff was called.
A crowd assembled.
The burglars' tools
were noted and catalogued.

A miracle! All cried
as thieves awoke
and were put in irons.

An eager friar
passing that way
on a pilgrimage,
reclaimed the precious
door-nails,
stuffed the torn gilding
into his mendicant bag,
and shuffled away.

The crowd moved
to the gallows' square
where Bishop Theodred
condemned all eight
to share a single gibbet.

A miracle! The crowd chants
as word of the failed robbery
spreads far and wide.
Saint Edmund saved himself!

Ah! moaned the eldest thief,
had we not
partaken of
that mushroom stew!

THE MYSTERIES
OF ELSDON CHURCHYARD

1
Why did the bell
of Elsdon Church
resound
across the landscape,

shaking the ground
of the tumulus mound
above the empty motte
of Elsdon Castle?

Why did the voice
of St. Cuthbert's minister
echo deep mystery
in even a commonplace
sermon, bass-deep
from a voice that was
no lower than baritone?

Thank the medieval
architect who thrust
three horses' skulls
upright into an oaken
cabinet,

a resonance box
suspended
within the bell-tower.

Bell above
thrice amplified below
and out across
the countryside;
preacher in pulpit
graced with the tone
of thunder-Jehovah.

2
Whose the stone
coffin that leans
against the wall
of St. Cuthbert's?

No one can move it,
and no one knows
what sacred corpse
reclined within its hollow,
sculpted to human
silhouette.

Monks, it was said,
came here with relics
of St. Cuthbert,
in flight from the Vikings,

but who could flee
cross-country
with a stone sepulchre
and the eight horses
and cumbersome cart
it would take to haul
an entire saint
and his equipage?

No, this was not Cuthbert
whose tomb
rests finally in Durham,
but some unknown knight,
perhaps, who willed
himself a mighty coffin
where neither rat nor worm
could mar his godlike
features —

Yet what is left?
Lidless, leaning
against a wall
where dogs and derelicts
can lift a leg,

flesh, armor and bones
all gone, a hollow
in human outline,
no man and
Everyman.

3
Before Elli's Valley
became "Elsdon,"
before the invading
Vikings,
before the Normans,
who built Elsdon Castle
before the Saxons,
guttering the Anglish
tongue, Romans
lived here and prospered,
secure in their reign
amid their household
and temple gods.

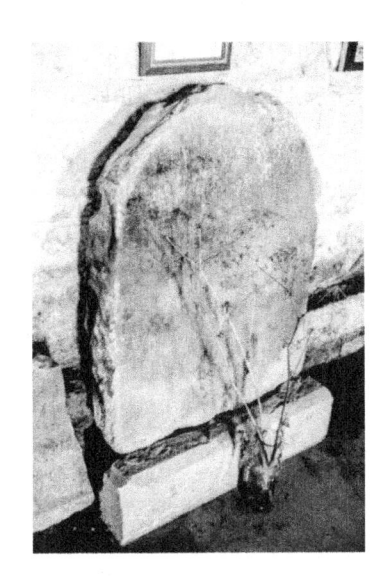

Here, against the unwilling
walls of Saint Cuthbert's
a Roman gravestone.

To the divine Manes,

he of the prefect
of the first cohort
of the Augustan of the Lusitani,
also of the second cohort
of the Breuci, subcurator
of the Flaminian Way
and of the distribution
of maintenance
subcurator of public works.

Julia Lucilla had this erected
to her husband well deserving.
He lived forty-eight years
six months and five days.

Pushed back southward
from the Antonine Wall
to Hadrian's Wall, then out
of Britain altogether
as barbarians swarmed Europe,
Romans left only stones,
deep-buried Lares and Penates
(their household gods)
beneath their houses,
the envied ruins
of colossal baths, the heads
and torsos of toppled gods.

Still, every English ghost
looks out to sea
for the dreaded Viking sails,
and treads lightly, lest
a Roman hand reach up
to seize its ankle.

Turn any stone
and a face looks up.

RAVENS ARE WAITING, THE CROWS HAVE ARRIVED

1
Ravens are waiting. The crows have arrived.
Brown oaks darken with their spread wings, fanned tails.
Shrill calls from inside the chapel belfry
echo from the building fronts — a census
might count a thousand; how many make up
one "murder" is anyone's guess, but this,
at edge of college campus, counts as
a university already robed,
their corvine dissertations defended,
their *gaudeamus* anthems sunset-sung
as they spatter the bus-shelter's rooftops
and huddle all night in their unseen nests,
where they are nurturing tomorrow's crows
for their ancient calling. Ravens are waiting,
edged out, biding their time in ones and twos,
but they, too, are about their business,
hatching as many eggs as possible,
for they, afloat the white tide of Europe
onto this new continent, remember.

2
Adapted from The Anglo-Saxon Chronicle, 937 CE

Here at Brunanburh, hosts
killed by King Athelstan,
lord of long-armed earls,
boon-giver of bracelets
to kneeling nobles,
killed he countless ones,
and with his brother also
Edmund, Elder, the aetheling —
how many killed? Too many
to count! Down the dead fell
as they destroyed the dread Scots
and burned their fair-sailed ships.

Loud the field resounded, bright
as gold the sweat on their armor!
Glad the sun rose, giving
light, the great star's morning
merry over the field of blood.
Dead soldiers lay, with lance
and dart struck down,
Norsemen prostrate
their brazen shields behind,
from arrows overshot.
Or Viking, or Scot,
or trait'rous Briton ally,
died they all dead
beneath the same bright sky!

Though some escaped,
Norsemen fleet in their nailed ships,
dragged off with our darts
inside them, sailed off
on the stormy sea
to fight a better day —
let them flee to Dublin,
sad city in Viking thrall!

But bellowing berserkers
they left behind.
Let them enjoy the crows,
and keening for their kind,
the dismal, starving kite
to entrail feast invite,
and let their last sight
be the black raven
with his horned beak
descending wide-winged.
And they, of armor stripped,
invite the white worm,
the voiceless toad,
the maggot-bearing fly.
By mid-day sun, the blood-
feast will draw the eagle,

and the greedy after-feast
of the falcon, battle-hawk.
At dusk, the gray beast comes.
Let but one live lamenting
the jaws of the wood-wolf.

Never in all the world's war
had there been a greater
slaughter, nor more destroyed
by the sharpened sword!

3
These are not bombs or arrows, yet.
Those who walk vertical are not yet
horizontal and motionless.
Not javelins, but hurled epithets,
anonymous death threats
are their weapons of choice.

Passive, unvaccinated idiots,
four to a pram, wheel to the park,
pushed by unlettered parents
whose only book celebrates
eyes plucked for eyes unopened.

The earth beneath them weeps,
the methane-pocketed soil shrugs,
Swiss-cheese sink-holed hollowed:
whose house will it swallow next?

The water, oil-slicked, rills bright
in rainbow glitterings, but no one
minds. The bees, too weak to pollinate
the trees, can only buzz protest.
The shrinking bird host
has no elected legislators.

The armies are everywhere.
More bullets in stock than ever
babies can be made. One with
your name on it awaits you!
Just one emergency more,
and troops tip-toe
across this border, that
river declared as mine
and not yours, the oil there
for the taking, loot's prime
directive! A subtle lead-up,
dueling conspiracies of complicit
foreigners, expert at poisoning
from village well to townhouse
door-knob, gas-death for all,
warehouses at the ready, germs known
and unknown packed up
for easy distribution. War-mongers
worse than war-hawks, with
mercenary wink, a profit
pocketed, the rich secured
in their walled manors —
oh, they are almost ready!

Led by a drooling madman,
and a sniveling weasel, a nation rots.
No need for foreign enemies
when enemies of the people
are among us already. Take arms!
The National Guard will help.
Your local police are militarized
and know who the secret Muslims are!

Park and field, tent city
and commandeered stadium,
vast open spaces sky-spread
await the arrival of carrion.
The ground will groan
with the bodies of the dead.
Serves them right: journalists

the scum of Karl Marx, the host
of homeless (what business theirs
to clog our cities?), those bearded
zealots with their hairy Protocols,
off with you, o everything but white!

Athelstan's heirs, they cannot wait
for this. They were born to see
this thing through at last.
Sheets off, gentlemen, it's
Armageddon among us.

Ravens are waiting.
The crows have arrived.

THE DEVELOPER

After the 11th-century Anglo-Saxon

Even before your birth
this home was built for you.
Your sculpted form was carved
to adorn its courtyard
even before your mother bore you.
We have planned for everything:
how many floors, how deep the lot.
(These things are not determined
until I bring you to it.
Imagine not having to worry
about room enough for all
those honors and possessions!)

Here, in this vestibule remain,
until I measure you
and the matching sod of earth.
The ceiling is too low, you say?
It is not highly built.
"Unhigh" or "low" are just two ways
to look at today's economies
of scale and space.
Too low to stand, yes, yes,
too narrow for arm-swing.

I am here for you. See here:
the roof is built just up
to the breast's proud swell,
and no further. Horizontal?
A matter of perspective,
of marketing and branding.

In fact, we have everything ready.
I wanted to surprise you. Right here
you shall dwell full cold,
in dimness and darkness,
hearth-black, a cauldron cold
with, shall we say honestly,
an air of putrefaction.

Your new house needs no door
(a flat stone, a quaint barrow
of piled rocks for that pagan look),
nor is is lit within. Go in,
and feel yourself detained
in windowless darkness. Never
again will you need a house-key,
no phone, no lamp, no keeping out
your new neighbors, the creeping
and crawling things who just cannot
wait to make your acquaintance.
The worms come round
for breakfast, lunch *and* dinner.

You have no need of friends.
They will not come, anyway,
not after the feasting, songs,
and fights over your belongings —
save for that one who digs,
opens the earth-top remembering
your strong arms, your kisses,
or, more likely, that golden finger-
ring he did not dare remove,

and seeing you at home this way,
he shall sicken and drop
the midnight shovel, for you
shall have become loathsome,
even to the sun and stars.

I take no fee for this.
Death am I, and I have done my due.

ICELANDIC JUSTICE

*Adapted from the Old Norse,
   as found in Williams'* Gnomic Poetry

And he of you, one or the other
that shall rail against the settlement
of a dispute, or deny atonement made,
or break an oath he was bidden to swear:

Hunt him we shall, as we hunt the wolf,
to the far hills and the icy crevasse,
even to the mouth of Hel, wherever wolf
would flee, he we shall follow,
to the earth's last Christian church we hunt him,
even in the heathen place of offerings
we shall hunt and find him;

we shall seek him as far as fire burns,
to the last meadow where earth-grass greens,
to any place where sons their mother summon
to hearth-side, to the last mother's bearing
of the last son of her line we seek him,

at any place where any wanderer
kindles his lonely fire, we find him out,
to any sea that ships sail, to any isle
where the fugitive's shield shines
in a foreigner's battles, we know
his name and by his name we find him.

Can he find a place where no sun shines,
where no snow settles white on hillocks,
where waters lie flat with no fish-fin upon it,
where there is no shade or shard of fir
to give him shelter or kind kindling?

Oh, let him fly with a fair wind behind him!
Let him have winds of fame in his new-found name.
We shall find him out, as sure as sky turns,
as sure as the earth lets us walk upon it
and not sink down to quicksand, as sure as wind
blows sails, and waters go to the sea,
as long as one mean churl casts seed
into the earth at ice-break,
as long as there is bread to eat and mead
to comfort our long-arm quest,
he shall not evade the Law!

MOVING TO PROVIDENCE, 1985

This is Providence when it was still rather a hell-hole, but a very cheap place for writers to live. I moved there with my Siamese cat in 1985 and had eleven rooms in a Victorian house, for $450 a month. The unofficial state motto was "Mobsters and Lobsters" and the natives were exceedingly unfriendly. I lived there three years before I ever set foot in another person's house. I just found these poetic journal entries describing how awful it was, or seemed to be. For inexplicable reasons, I would spend almost half of my adult years in New England.

> I have moved to Providence,
> a writer's paradise of low rents and large spaces.
> The natives speak a dialect of broken English
> conjugated with expletives. I have never heard
> so many Fs and mother-F's on a city bus.
>
> They drive outdated cars, wide as bombers,
> paint-scraped and dented,
> leprous with rust-spot camouflage
> turn corners with daring and macho screeches,
> black trails of tires at every corner.
>
> Boys at the corner loiter for cars, hand men
> those little bags of powder they crave
> as they furtively leave the off-ramp
> for our disreputable neighborhood.
> That the bags are full of baking powder
> they will only learn later as even boys
> know well the rules of cheat and sharp trading.
>
> Eight of ten voters are Catholic.
> Virgins in little inverted bath-tubs adorn
> the house fronts of the treeless side streets.
> An old man tells me, "No trees. No birds.
> No squirrels. No nuts. No leaves to rake."

The heads of state and their families
control unmeasured tracts of property.
The governor's name and picture adorn
each monolith and highway ramp.
Each sign must include "His Excellency"
before the current felon's proper name.

The marble capitol is large enough
    to detain, if necessary,
      the entire electorate.

Well-known gangsters reside discreetly,
unperturbed by warrants or searches.
One tip-toes past the vending machine
storefront, the funeral home, the house
of the respected grandmother "of that name."

Free enterprise is encouraged, narcotically.
Homes of the Anglo-rich are frequently burgled.
On a hill, the prestigious University
trains the sons of the rich
to assume their places of power.
The city is full of history, devoid of culture.
It drove out Poe, and tolerated Lovecraft
while watching him slant and starve.

It imports insults and toxic waste,
exports the simulacrum of itself:
cobblestones and shuttlecocks,
andirons and lightning rods and tassled shawls,
a horse, a red hen, a barrel of molasses
fresh from the Triangle trade.

The natives are known for aloofness,
their way of sidestepping foreigners.
Only family are invited to dinner.
Young men leave the state
to find a girl who isn't a cousin.
One must be introduced to a prostitute.

Despite all this, the artists come here.
Cheap is cheap. Besides, where else
can you find a Third World Country
without leaving New England?

GERTRUDE AND THE REVENANT

*A Heathen tale of the Danes
made Christian, but just barely.*

First and fairest — virgin maid —
in all the realms of Charlemagne,
to her from far and near the plea
came, Help us, saint and prophetess!

Godfather but newly dead, left
to Gertrude alone his towers.
Red the banners boldly blazoned,

but in time there came a count,
envious-eyed with armed minions
to spoil and waste the land about,

until the proud tower, prey
to malice and treason, fell.
By secret way and cavern, she

alone escaped their ravages.
Of all her silks and jewels, none
were left to her. One staff and book

was all she took upon her pilgrim
way, not to the Emperor, not
to some neighbor lord for succor,

but to the graveyard cold and drear,
where, striking her staff inside the tomb
and opening her book of elder lore,

she read a chapter to open the way,
another more for the summoning,
a third to name the awakened dead.

Loud she read, the wind her clamor,
the thunder her drum, the owl
her oboe shrill and quickening,

until the dead man heard her song.
With moan as deep as mountain
echo, up rose the shaggèd head

of one she knew but all too well
(in horror she averted eye
from the rotted sockets' glare).

"Who dares with ancient lore
and cursed magic to summon me?"
the gelid thing now roared.

Upon her knees she fell, a-tremble.
"Refuse me not, 't is I, Gertrude,
god-daughter and heir, 't is I,

who, kneeling, implore your ghost,
for none alive can aid me.
To a count unknown to me

the gates were thrown, the walls
fell undefended, tower to cellar
looted, the women ravished.

The peasants groan, their corn,
not even a seed for planting,
has been carried off by one

who honors neither law nor custom,
but takes whatever his arm
can seize. The monks are fled,

the village bells are silent. Soon
snow will come, and all will starve.
Help me, god-father dear!"

And hearing this, the stone
above the corpse was pushed aside,
The walls of the vault exploded.

Stood he on his long legs strong,
flesh-rot returned to sinew,
godly grew his arms and shoulders.

Went they the maid and skeleton
back to the tower by line of sight,
trees sundered, tombs toppled,

streams forded whether or no
the waters favored, on they went,
until the towers' doors he rent.

The living courtiers crept away,
the traitorous followers fled,
even the bartered, ill-used wives.

Gone they were like dew of dawn.
Only the Count stood firm.
He laughed at Gertrude and the shade.

"You, Revenant, I fear you not,"
he said, not putting down his cup.
"I am a warrior proven strong

"and you are only a skeleton.
Come forth and match me
hand for hand, and here I stand

"swordless and defy you.
This tower and all its fiefs
are mine, stone to straw."

Slow he moved with dead man's gait,
dead heart pulsing in vacant
rib-cage, and then the skeleton

was upon him, "*One*," he said,
as bony hands gripped
the warrior's belt and tunic.

"For this tower is mine!"
Arms wrapped a waist
more fit for feast than fighting

and raised him a-high. A snap
and a cry, and his spine was twain.
"*Two*! For the scoured land!"

Thrust up again, the rag-doll
ruffian was seized at knees,
and both snapped as saplings

give way to the broad-axe.
"*Three!* For thou hast offended
a woman not only of grace

and beauty, but witching ways!
Beware the woman with rod
and book, who keens the wind

and raises the angry dead
to avenge her." That said,
the skeleton collapsed

and never more spoke, nor
walked of it own accord, nay,
not even a whisper uttered.

That eve, the bones took up
she into a burlap sack,
and Gertrude, shunning all,

carried her burden sore
to the sundered tomb, and laid
bone by bone into his bed

the beloved godfather,
then from a rose bloomed
out of season, she plucked

three petals, and kneeled
and prayed to whatever
it was she believed in.

And the earth closed up,
and the tomb walls righted,
and the toppled cross

returned to its place
above the doorway.
She built a great church.

The grateful folk filed in
to see its gilded roof
and hear the chastened monks

sing *Te Deum laudaumus*,
over the silent bones,
and Gertrude, silent, smiled.

DOMITIAN'S BLACK ROOM

Do you know who I am?
Do you know what this place is?
Bribe-takers, slave rapers, virgin-
abductors, temple defilers, daughter
seducers, wine adulterers, slum-
owning generators of a thousand
vices, some yet to be named!
I am Domitian, your *Emperor!*
Kneel and abase yourselves.
Your *God!* (I see that all
but three are on their knees.

Look how they grovel!) A hug,
Martius, and Gemellus, and Titus.
You smile and stand, you get
the joke. What is this place?

In the rest come now,
two by two through the black
corridor to greet me,
now that my "temple oracle"
voice has died away.

Marus, I see you have soiled your toga!
Go off to the side there and get another.
What, Senator, no mirthful greeting?
(Just watch as all the old men's
remaining teeth light up
as they invent forced grins, watch next
as their hands lift up the folds of robes
to ease the coming bows and curtseys.)

Down to your knees, I see,
as if to beg pardon, no doubt for all
that I have agreed to know, yet overlook.
Up! Up! Was the way well-lit?

Did torches fail to reflect
the black hues of jet and onyx?
Did you perspire to near fainting
as you passed the grates
through which you viewed
my room of sharpened axes?

Ha! I heard some count aloud
how many steps they descended
as you came down to reach me.

Your protests were noted
when your own guards
were replaced by my Praetorians.
Spotting a soldier he knew,
our friend Vitruvius offered
his tender bottom if only they'd let
him go back to his villa
afterwards. He'll join us soon
once ten Praetorians,
have had their way with him.

Whatever bribes you gave
from your purses, those rings
and armlets, I'll pile them up
and find some better use
than the adornment of reprobates.

Not in your life have any of you
been this far below the ground.
There are things down here
that even the Etruscans dread.
Did you hear the hard rush
of the Tiber waters,
the groan of the Cloaca Maxima
as you passed below the rat-filled deep?

I heard one say the word "Avernus."
Every word echoes down to me —
everything! I heard one mumbled
Nazarene prayer, but not who uttered it.
Dream on of Hell and Hades:
I am down here awaiting you.
You are the first to come
to the Black Room of Domitian.
I will summon others after you.
There are lists! There are lists!

Stop that wailing and murmuring now!
Ring that gong over there!
Again! They hear us! They stir!
The iron doors groan open
(a nice effect, I must say,
and look at some of them, fainting!)

Eheu, what is this place? Look up,
you sniveling millionaires
and Senators. It is *dinner*!
Ha! *Ha!* *Ha!* Ha! Ha! Ha! Ha!

I DREAMT I WAS THE APENNINES

I dreamt I was the Apennines, a thousand miles
of me from Liguria to Reggio, on to my toe-hold
across the water in Sicily. I was so large
that a cloud-front was but a single breath
into my caverned lungs. My sleep withheld
the fury of volcanos, the wrath of avalanche.
I hoard one tiny glacier to ice my summer fever.

Then Zeus came back in his dark thundercloud —
welcome after so many centuries of slumber —
to tell me his temple had been restored in Athens
and that a sacrificial fire now burned anew,
to the despair of the bearded Orthodox.

He brought me a great earthquake. Ah,
I wanted it to go on forever. All the way
to Rome, they will be feeling my fervor.
Let Paris burn, and Lisbon shudder!
Down, Babylon — Atlantis, sink!
Rise, seas, above Poseidon's head!
Look at them running, the little ants!
Tyrants and breakers of oaths, flee
from your shabby brickwork assemblies!

Now that I am awakened, I summon
the poets, musicians, painters, and madmen.
Come to the Abruzzi and its sheltering peaks,
where the secret police will never find you.
Come to my untamed forests beneath,
where the Italian wolf still suckles Romulus,
and where the brown bear alone abides.
Forte e gentile, mountains of bandits,
hide-out of excommunicated patriots,
refuge of Partisans disguised as shepherds.

I dreamt I was the Apennines,
and one day I will walk to Rome
with boulders as my sandals, mendicant
to bring the stones of Chthonic temples back,
halls of dark serpentine ophiolite,
to rest upon the stones of the Nazarene.

These things take time. A volcano
would help to move my plans along.
I will tread on landslide, mudslide and flood.
Sink holes will be my footprints, but I will come.
Mountains are more patient than clouds,
more full of purpose than the churning sea.
Tremble, Rome, before my bells of stone!

THE OLD BRICK HOUSE AT CARPENTERTOWN

Only a few memories define it
now that it is gone, gone
to the last brick, a place
where two roads meet
in a bramble of scrub trees
and blackberries wild.

Never turn on the lights
in the dining room.
If you flick the switch,
you smell smoke
and hear a crackling sound
somewhere behind
the peeling wallpaper.

Never go down those steps
to the cellar. The rats
are there, and they own it.

Tap water is only
for taking a bath.
It is not safe to drink;
the well is poisoned
by the slow seep
of wet ash-piles
from the glowing coke-ovens.

Never go up
to the slanted attic whose one
sole window throws light
one hour a day
on the head and shoulders
of a nameless Greek.

Do not eat the dog's
worm medicine,
even if it looks like
M&Ms.

Never tell anyone
you have learned to levitate
and do not need to touch
foot to stair-tread
coming down from your bedroom.

Never tell anyone
ever again
about your imaginary
playmate. Just lie
and say you were alone.
Both voices were yours.
Smile mysteriously.

When, late at night,
you press your face
to a window pane
and an escaped black panther,
paws on the window-sill,
regards you eye-to-eye,
tell no one.

When a great storm
comes, run to the porch
to feel the rain-lash
against your face.
Welcome the lightning.
Imagine yourself as one
of the Lombardy poplars
aching for a thunderbolt.

Carry its many rooms
inside you forever,
haunter of your own
haunted house.

THE WINNER

Damn if he didn't beat the odds!

John won the lottery.
He spent all night
listing the things he'd do
as soon as the cash
filled his house to the rafters.

Running downtown
to find a lawyer,
crosswalk-waiting
at Fifth and Smithfield

(not taking any chances
with his hundreds
of millions!)

he was struck
by a falling meteorite,
a fireball so hot
he was sublimed
to a dirt-brown cloud
that instantly dispersed.

Crowds edged
the sinkhole crater,
wondering who ...

THE TIMES THAT BURN THE BRAIN

The times that burn the brain are few:
when art commands that love be shed;
when you last hope to see the dead,
now truly gone, come into view;

when abstract thoughts become mere breath
upon the tongue, and Liberty
lies down with chains and musketry;
when you admit that gainless death

burns thousands from a tyrant brain
and murder stains your nation's face,
as one by one the storms erase
all freedoms in a bloody rain;

to climb a hill before the dawn
and find your heart's last village lost
into the concrete void of time,
to know the past is now beyond
your step, yourself a wordy ghost,
unchanging captive in a rhyme.

—1973, rev. 2019.

A WING OF TIME

This little "Twilight Zone" episode narrative poem has me going back in time in 1973, revisiting the college town where I lived from 1965 to 1969. Ironic now that I felt "so much older."

This village street will always split me —
    half in the gray-fringed present,
    half quarked away in time
from dull today to that brilliant
    yesterday — a day I am not yet
      twenty and the maples seem shorter,
        the houses whiter, the sky
a bluer blue through eyes unclouded.

I stand before a dingy storefront.
Back then it was a dress shop
    with but a single mannequin.
Next to it was Gorman's
    steamy laundromat
churning students' underwear and towels,
a nickel-dime-quarter juggernaut
devouring stray socks, a treasury
of lint and buttons.

Above the laundry, beyond that rotting
window-frame, was my first apartment.
Was it fifteen dollars a month I paid
for two converted office rooms,
    a hallway bathroom and shower?
Are those the same curtains still,
tattered and colorless as I found them
and left them? The same glass,
certainly, through which I watched
the leaf-fall, lightning, snowstorm,
the neon light of the Hotel Bar
(no one under twenty-one admitted!)

I see the pale green painted wall
not changed in grudging landlord years.
I climb the narrow stairs, pass down
the beer-corroded corridor to my door,
whose frosted glass was once gold-leafed
with some insurance agent's name.

Do I do this? Are my hands, nervous,
solid enough to knock, or am I dreaming?
My tap on the glass is solid enough.
A thin blond woman answers, puzzled.
I tell her I lived here as a student,
    oh, many years ago.
Could I just stand here a moment,
look out her window at the village green? —

where someone, in unintended irony,
has placed the town's own name
in giant wooden letters,
    as though the inhabitants
    needed to be reminded,
the traveler admonished.
Sinners, this is Edinboro!
Fathers, guard your daughters!

A wave of heat rolls through the trees outside.
Were it a wing of Time, whose darker side
enfolds the past, what memories appear?
I see the vanished store whose wooden frame
extends into the square, a blur of green
as sycamores sawed down or thunderstruck
burst back to view. A sigh of life unfurls,
the lake regains its water lily bloom,
long-dead sparrows rebuild forgotten nests,
and on the street, departed friends go by —

Squat Bertha goes to get her mail. Next door,
her restaurant slides to bankruptcy,
unpaid employees and a sheriff's sale.
I heard her scold her harried waitresses

for wasting moldy pie. *Do it like this!* —
she flipped the pie-slice over deftly
then scraped a knife across the furry crust,
flipping it back to who would ever know —
now serve it with a smile! Above her store,
she had her quart of beer, remembering
the brothel she ran in her Erie days.
The men in her rooms are boarders, students.
Deans and professors eat at her table.
Head high, she's almost respectable now.

I see four shadows in the alleyway —
three high school boys and a slow-minded girl.
She goes there often. They catch her there,
against the wall their prying hands adept
at raising her skirt, stealing quick pleasure.
After the shadows mingle, pressed on brick,
sneakered feet scatter in every direction.

Outside the bar, the college boys loitering
swoon as Jamie and her sketchpad pass them.
Her tied-back hair jet black, her almond eyes
Eurasian orbs of challenge and surrender.
Her breasts move through their dreams
     like wrecking cranes.
Her siren silhouette, voice-song, Muse-call,
perfect things, untouchably sufficient.
It was enough that she existed here.

Now others pass: a student prince who died
in megalo-brainfire tumor madness;
the tragic bronchial artist coughing,
imagining consumption's early death;
one, two, a half dozen for Vietnam,
whose jungles would cripple them, or kill them
(one whose body was never found, looks up
as though his ghost and my vision had locked);

my best friends, the mad and sad ones, strolling
on by as though I still awaited them —
the best of their time, the dreamer drop-outs,
acid, depression, poverty and war
cutting its swath through my generation.
In this interval a hundred have passed,
known and unknown, the loved and the yearned-for,
all of them still before their beginnings,
not drinking the poison of compromise,
not marrying lies, denying visions,
not using youth to engender monsters.
They do not see my future looking down,
not one of them seems coarse or mediocre.

And there, impossibly, I see myself,
a younger form, approach.
He is by all standards, pretty much
    out of his mind.
His eyes are wide with poems.
He turns and looks back at passers-by
if they happened to have beautiful eyes.
He is carrying a batch
   of his underground newspaper
    giving them out
      to everyone he recognizes.
He enters through the door below,
his footsteps sure upon the stair.
I turn, I dash into the darkened hall.
I hide in the bathroom until he passes,
then tread my way silently
to the street, and to the present.

He only cares about the future.
I wish I could warn him.
I think he was very foolish
   to linger here,
as I was foolish to return.

Yet this is what I learned:
I always thought others the meteors,
racing on by, too hot to touch,
never quite seen or palpable.
I thought the world a-spin
away and beneath my grasp,
yet here it sits, slow in its orbit
as a banana slug.
And now I understand:
I was the meteor. I am the meteor.
I blaze through. Nothing remains
of me but these etched words.

HITHER AND YON

There is one who loves me,
   three towns hither,
and there is one I love,
   just three towns yon.
Yet over all of us one hand
has painted the same starry vault
that rotates just the same;
the trees have turned the same
resplendent gold,
   but the veined and crispèd leaves
   are not the same here
   as they are hither and yon.
The same moon goes new to gibbous
   here, and then full to gibbous again
   until there is no moon above us,
dark here, dark hither, dark yon.
Not one of us can reach out to touch
from our closed rooms the same dawn.
We will shiver a common winter.
We will sleep singly, or not at all,
wasting with pent-up longing.
In sad fact, not one of us
shall ever see the other again.

—1973, rev. 2019.

THE DAEMON LEADS ME ON

Greece, when thy fleet-footed Hermes graced
my adolescence with the poet's tongue,
when eyes conceived of impossible art
and the sightless, deaf and immutable
logic of words first sprung to my grasp;
even when music burst upon me —
in all that beauteous conception
no word or chord attained this pitch
where now I lie.

Earth, now that your dew-time's herald larks
have urged the hesitant spring of the sun,
I wake to hold one, new to my arms
as our restless and irrefutable
tokens of lips, caresses and sighs
carry us over the cavernous edge
of frozen sea.

Thanos, when thy hungry gravebed takes
my poems, and this human eye
grows black with dreaming and weeping
    for art,
and a carpet of green and spurious twigs
drains my old cells in bloodless symmetry,
will this love be coin enough for the boatman?
will whom I loved suffice to keep my name
and poems read?

Hermes has been my guide.
I know nothing of grace or immortality.
The god of sudden inspiration
is my daemon, and I must pay him
by being buffeted this way, that way,
one step ahead of the landlord,
at odds with order and decency until I am
of words bereft.

                                                — *1973, rev. 2019.*

1796 EDINBORO LAKE

Off the Venango path and north
of the place called Cussewago, they found
the uninhabited lake. What did it look like then?
It was crammed to its edge with ancient trees
a woods in perpetual dusk where one
could walk for three days before
another cabin smoked out in a clearing.
Here and there along the way
some rotted, roofless ruin lay
where an Erie long-house had been,
or a mound mysterious full of arrow-heads,
a place whose people had vanished,
driven by the Canada's enraged Hurons
into extinction. No more Eries, no more
this lake a place of winter refuge.
It was empty, and waiting.

So why not claim it? Why not this lake,
so like the lochs of Scotland, why not
this man, John Culberston, Scot-born
but free? From Philadelphia west
he had come; he had weathered out
that Britain-versus-America problem
and it was time to put down roots.
Why not this kettle lake, carved out
of the underlying rock by the glaciers?
The Indian, a Mingo, had told him

about this place, and called it
Conneautee. So here it was,
just as the guide had promised,
a placid little loch just half a mile
across, with pines enough around
to build a town, flat land for grain,
and for the grist mill he would build;
for grain and whisley were the way
to wealth. "What think
you, wife?" he asked his silent consort.
Jeanette took in the sweep of clouds,
the sky-enfolding blue waters, watched
as a flock of crows cawed and winged
welcome. "I like it," she said.
The half-naked Indian grunted.
If he knew more about the place,
he said nothing. The dark swamp
nearby was well concealed by trees
and the nodding cat-tails. (No need
to upset them about what lived there
and how no one slept well
on certain nights when sorrow
rose like a beast from the bottom!)
Man, woman, horses and wagon
stood for a long time, the little clouds
of their breathing in chill air
as calm as a peace pipe.
Everything they owned,
    they had dragged here.

Down at the lake-edge
their shiny boots ground
time-worn gravel beneath them.
They knew nothing of Ice Ages,
departing glaciers and porous
limestone. They did not know
how shallow the soil was, how brief
the growing season, how deep

the snows piled on in winter,
a place where frost came in August
and snow remained till May.

Still, nothing could be worse
than Scotland: this they would say
on all the winter nights to come.

They canoed to the north, reed grass
and full of inlets, fish abounding,
fens buried in mists, tall pines bent
and fallen to the earth. Something
had walked here unhappily, storms
called down in its anger. Pray
that its time has come and gone!

Pools dank with toads alternated
with blue patches herons favored.
Fog started there, it seemed.
The dusk-mist that rose
around them thickened.
Only the warm spot of sunglow
guided them back again.

And then they found the creek,
the lake's shallow outlet,
good land on either side
for houses, a place to dam up
and run his mill. All good,
it seemed. "This is home,"
he said to his wife, "now
and for all the time we have left."

"There's no church," she worried.
"Oh, churches will come," he answered.
"There will be no stopping them."
"What shall we call the place?"
"Edinburgh." He said. "The only city
worth its name in all of Scotland."

The sun set, the swamp exhaled
its methane-rich vapors, the frogs
began their melancholy chorus.
Back at the lake-edge vantage,
they made their tent, their fire
the first that the land had seen
in over a hundred years.

They did not dream that night,
but something in and under them
dreamt of their lives and deaths,
their burials on this very ground,
the slow seep of waters upwards,
an inverse sun rising
in the names of their children to come.

—1973, rev. December 2019.

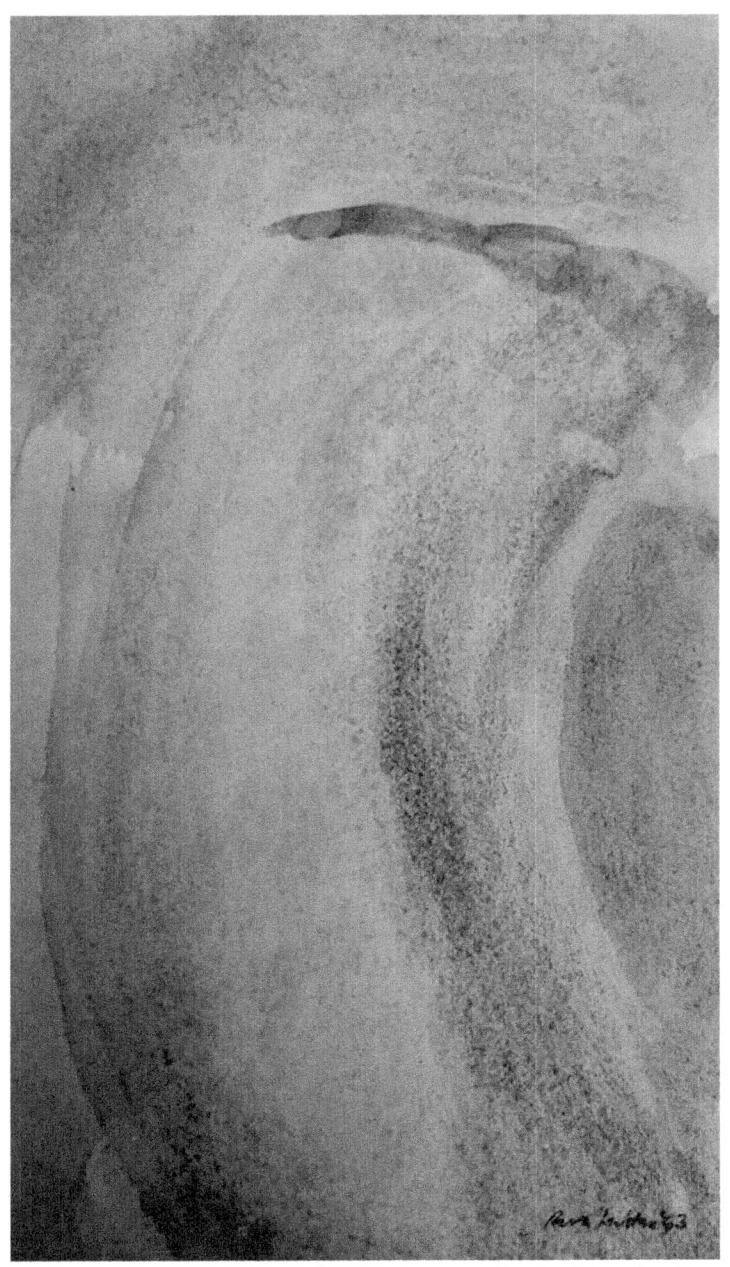

Original watercolor by Riva Leviten.

THE MIDNIGHT IBIS

after a watercolor by Riva Leviten

On this foggy night, any river
    could be the Nile
and that dark thing afloat
    could be the crocodile
that let the Moses-basket
    pass on by,
and laughed about it still
    with weepless eye.

There is a hooked-head shape
    arc'd like a scythe
with one bright orb that might
    be the isolate ibis, lithe
and tomb-art motionless.

Or it might be nothing,
    a sight not solid
an unnamed form made up
    of arc and column,
now gray on white, now white
    on gray,
cloud-tuft, fog breath dispersed.
    Sometimes it is the eye
that thinks a thing — sometimes
    it is the mind that sees!

Ibis! the very totem-form of Thoth,
who gave the art of writing to Ani
(the first known scribe), your beak
suggesting stylus on paper roll,
chisel on somnolent basalt, hand-wave
of words to outlive the burning stars.

Ibis! watcher! listener! father
of cartouche and hieroglyph,
unsmiling arbiter of line and rhyme.
Ibis thou swift messenger of dreams,
of waking-moment revelation
of the impossibly true or to-be-true
(Hermes to the blue-skied Greeks),
your truth that fleeting visions,
unless inscribed, are gone like fog,
word-foam on a tideless sea.

—Feb 9, 2017

THE MARCH TO THE SCAFFOLD

after the music of *Symphonie Fantastique* of Berlioz

Today I die in Paris, city of demons and hideous women.
What faces, replete with mustaches and hairy warts;
and what noses, what puffed-out cheeks,
    what crenelated mouths!
How tall is the shaft of the guillotine?
    How tall is the spire of Notre-Dame? The same!
The immensity of my crime, the same !
The amputated veterans of the Grand Army,
    the shoeless orphans, the cripples,
    stand in line in the gutters.
The rosette window darkens, the gargoyles sneer and gossip,
    the blind organist plays the *Dies Irae*.
A muffled bell mourns me.
    Laugh, hunchback, laugh, as you call out my death!
The chorus girls from the Opera rush the tumbrel wagon
    of the condemned.
Among them floats the spectre of the one I loved.
They lift her. Her arms are bare,
    smeared with the cemetery's black soil.
Stones they hurl at me, and excrement, and curses.
Their cruel missiles have broken my fingers.
    Ah! I shall not write again!
Wheels turn, the drum-roll of the ceremony
    becomes louder to my ears.
Old friends of my youth
    somewhere are singing the Marseillaise,
    too late, too far away.
One "*Ça ira*" and the wigged judge
    would be the one to die, not me!
Oh, had I but loved the Just and the True,
    instead of *her*.
Ah! The dread hour comes. The tumbrel stops.
    Rudely they push me forward.
I count the steps to the scaffold.
    Twelve, no, thirteen! Thirteen steps!

I wave away the priest.
    I pay no mind to the recitation of my crimes.
I demand to die in the Chinese manner:
    I will face the heavens.
Even the executioner shudders,
    but then he smiles and agrees.
How very novel! How like a poet!
The spectral woman faints with horror.
    My mother averts her eyes.
I see two vertical lines,
    an angle gleaming bright,
        some clouds.
Because I loved her,
    because she abandoned me,
        because she died —
Because —
    the blade! It descends!
Because —
    It descends!
Because I killed her.
Ah!

MARCHE AU SUPPLICE

Aujourd'hui je meurs à Paris.
    Ville des démons et des femmes hideuses!
Quels visages, remplis de moustaches et de verrues velues;
    et quels nez, quelles joues gonflées,
        quelles bouches crénelées!
Quelle est la hauteur de l'arbre de la guillotine?
Quelle est la hauteur de la flèche de Notre-Dame? La même!
L'immensité de mon crime, la même!
Les vétérans amputés de la Grande Armée,
    les orphelins sans sabots,
        les estropiés, font la queue dans les gouttières.
La fenêtre rosace s'assombrit,
    les gargouilles ricanent et bavardent,
    l'organiste aveugle joue le *Dies Irae*.
Une cloche étouffée me pleure.
    Riez, bossu, riez, que vous appelez ma mort!
Les filles de choeur de l'Opéra se précipitent
    vers le chariot du condamné.
Parmi elles flotte le spectre de celle que j'aimais.
   Ils la soulèvent.
  Ses bras sont nus,
    enduit de terre noire du cimetière.
  Des pierres,
    des excréments
        et des malédictions, ils me lancent.
Les missiles cruels m'ont cassé les doigts.
      Ah! Je n'écrirai plus!
Les roues tournent, le tambour de la cérémonie
    devient plus fort à mes oreilles.
Quelque part, de vieux amis de ma jeunesse
    chantent la Marseillaise,
      mais trop tard, trop loin.
Un «Ça ira« et le juge sévère
    celui qui mourrait, pas moi.
Oh, si j'avais aimé le Juste et le Vrai,
    au lieu d'elle.

Ah! L'heure de la terreur arrive.
       Le tumbrel s'arrête.
       Ils me poussent brutalement en avant.
Je compte les escaliers jusqu'à l'échafaud.
       Il y en a douze, non, treize!
            Treize escaliers!
Je refuse le prêtre.
       À la récitation de mes crimes, je n'écoute pas.
J'exige de mourir à la chinoise:
       Je ferai face au ciel.
Même le bourreau frémit,
       mais ensuite il sourit et accepte.
Quelle nouveauté! Comme un poète!
La femme spectrale s'évanouit d'horreur.
       Ma mère détourne les yeux.
Je voix deux lignes verticales,
       un angle brillant,
            quelques nuages.
Parce que je l'aimais,
       parce qu'elle m'a abandonné,
            parce qu'elle est morte,
   Parce que —
       la lame! Ça descend!
Parce que —
       Ça descend!
Parce que je l'ai tuée.
            Ah!

DANCE OF THE WITCHES' SABBATH

Adapted from Victor Hugo's La Ronde du Sabbat, 1825

Just as in a mystery, behold now
how the moon veils itself in cloud
before the black monastery's walls!
Spreading its fright, the midnight spirit
passes, swaying twelve times where once
a bell tolled (no more!) in the unpeopled
belfry. Long resounding comes the noise,
the air shakes, the roll and rumble stifled
as if locked up beneath the bell itself.
A shadow, and silence falling — listen!
Who thrusts these clamors upon the quiet
night? Who casts these phantom lights?
Dear God! The ruined vaults, the jagged doors
seem to be enveloped by filaments of fire.

Do we not hear, where the boxwood branches dip
into the Holy Water, an agitated tide of waves,
a tiny troubled lake a-boil in its granite urn?
Commend our souls to those who look down
upon us! Down here, among the blue rays,
among the scarlet flames, with cries and songs,
with human sighs and inhuman barking,

    now everywhere, waters, mountains, woods,
larvae, dragons, vampires and gnomes,
monsters whose hell dreams only phantoms,
the witch, set free from the deserted tombs,
her silver birch broom whistling through air,
Necromancers tiara'd with mystical caps
above whom cabalistic symbols glow,
the no-nonsense demons, the crafty goblins,
all welcomed by the jagged line of roof,
by the broken hinge of the abandoned gate,
children of de-sanctified waste places come;
they come right through, a thousand lightnings,

the airy gaps in the stained-glass windows.
They enter the old cloister as a swirling wave.
He stands amid them, Lucifer, he, their Prince,
his bull's forehead concealed beneath
the high-capped miter of heavy iron.
The chasuble has veiled his diaphanous wings,
as on the crumbling altar he places his cloven foot.
O terror! Now they are singing, here in this place
where day and night the Eternal's eye should watch!
Now hand or claw reaches out for its kindred —
or, horror to behold, for nothing like itself —
they join, the form the immense circle,
the Antipode to the Cross, the bottomless!
Like a dark hurricane, the whirling begins.

To the eye that could not encompass the whole,
each hideous guest appears in his turn;
Hell spins, it seems, within the darkness,
its dreadful Zodiac all emblems of death.
The wind-force makes all fly, no need for wings!
They are carried 'round, and Satan conducts
the choral bursts of their beastly voices.

The dead
in their vaults below, if they could feel
beneath the paving stones, and hear this rout,
how they would tremble!

"Change partners randomly!"
As the demon mass around him rolls,
Satan and his joyful minions
press in on the altar and the Cross.
It is the cardinal night of autumn
The hour is solemn.

From Satan's fingers rise
the ancient flame that does not die,
that pale winged fluttering
fringed with the purple of kings —

*The dead
in their vaults below, if they could feel
beneath the paving stones, and hear this rout,
how they would tremble!*

"Yea, Children of Darkness,
rejoice in our triumph!
Brothers and Sisters, come
from a hundred dimensions,
from funereal places,
dens dank and deep.
Hell will escort you!
Come as a cohort
on griffin-powered
chariots! Come now!"

*The dead
in their vaults below, if they could feel
beneath the paving stones, and hear this rout,
how they would tremble!*

"We welcome deformity and crime!
Come without remorse,
goat-footed dwarfs and suicides!
Come, Ghouls, whose lips
have never weaned from carrion,
and the black blood of the dead.
Infernal women,
outdo your rivals
in lust and vengeance,
outlast your lovers
to the point of death
and join us, exultant!"

*The dead
in their vaults below, if they could feel
beneath the paving stones, and hear this rout,
how they would tremble!*

"Thrice-hounded Jews,
you are welcome among us!
Gypsies, Bohemians,
charged with anathema —
all may join us! Welcome!
Will o' the Wisps, we know you!
Pale specters who escaped by night
after an avenging patricide,
glide on the breeze, catch hold
of the frieze above the broken wall,
fly, or crawl!"

The dead
in their vaults below, if they could feel
beneath the paving stones, and hear this rout,
how they would tremble!

"Come, wicked goats,
eaters of everything.
Come, slender-bodied lice,
eaters of Everyman.
Come down, seducing Sylphs,
fall as a stream of hail,
and melting, bedew the field.
Take hands again, with one
of your own kind or kindred!
Follow the beat. Expand
the dance. Repeat the chants!"

The dead
in their vaults below, if they could feel
beneath the paving stones, and hear this rout,
how they would tremble!

"Now at this beautiful moment
experts in magic shine
in the orgy, their blood-red beards
puffed out with smoke and lightning.
What did you bring? What offering?
What innocent soul is your prey?

or better yet, what unsaved sinner
did you kidnap from a confessional?
The victim with a victim in his mouth!
The fire of evil craves them all!"

The dead
in their vaults below, if they could feel
beneath the paving stones, and hear this rout,
how they would tremble!

Laughing in the holy place
(for who would know?
who's watching there?
be still, if you would live to tell!)
Satan now parodies a chant
after Saint Matthew,
and in the chapel where his king
calls upon him, a demon sings
from the book of God!

The dead
in their vaults below, if they could feel
beneath the paving stones, and hear this rout,
how they would tremble!

"Bring them out of their resting place.
Open, ye tombs. Up, flagstones, up
lidded vaults! Bring out the monks
who once worshipped here. Arise!
And in each stall let a false monk spread
the fatal robe that burns his bones
and let a black chamberlain
attend to the burning of the cursed flame.

"Satan will see you now!
With your coarse hands
among the monk-dusk,
make ink and write,
Sorcerers, write your
Abracadabra!

"Fly away first, ye wild furred birds
of magic and curses,
dictate a whole new alchemy
of forbidden metals. Tear
the very fabric of matter to shreds!
This is what Satan is all about!
Fly away first, ye wild furred birds,
whose bald wings hang
from the alcoves of Smarra*
where the vampire dwells.

"Here is the signal!
Hell reclaims us.
The sun draws near! The time
may come when all souls know
no other flame than my black
lantern. May our dancing round
in the profound shadow
open the whole world
to an infernal circle!"

As I emerged from my hiding place
the pale dawn whitened the colossal
arches. Night and the Devil fled,
a confused swarm of dispersed demons.
And the dead, who had been burning bright
but moments before, reposed again.
The stones were back that held them;
their frozen glances gazing upward,
pillowed in ash and the dust of ages.

THE COLD WAVE, 1958

Slept on a church pew, walnut-hard
close enough to the still-hot radiator
she could roll up her thin cloth coat
to pillow her head. She licked cracked lips;
her numbed toes finally warmed. Three days
below zero and no sign of better to come!
She dreamt of a steam-hot kitchen, turkey
baking as in those long-gone Thanksgivings,
Charles and LeRoi anticipating
how much stuffing and sweet potatoes.

Lights red, lights blue, lights amber gold,
not from the Christmas tree past but from
the stained-glass morning sun-up
warming her face, oh! just an hour,
an hour longer rest; no one would know
how the unlocked Methodist Episcopal
had been her hotel for one night only.
She'd wash up in the bathroom below,
then come back up and give a nod to Jesus,
thank him out loud before she tip-toed
out to frozen ice-pack of sidewalk.

After what seemed only an eye-blink,
the windows were brighter, hotter,
and a hand poked at her shoulder
rudely. "Ma'am," a man's voice,
low like summer thunder on the hills'
other hollows, rumbled, "Ma'am, wake up."
Cora sat bolt upright, one hand tugged
down her long black skirt, the other across
her bosom, sliding away from where
the unwanted hand had prodded her.

The man's form changed, dark silhouette
to sun-paint, his white skin mosaic'd red
and blue and gold. His name was Ernest.
She knew him, and sometimes she mended
the clothes his mother brought over,
piecework she did for many in town.

"Ma'am," he told her, "You can't be sleepin' here.
It's not allowed." "Hmm," she muttered, and took
the coat and slowly unrolled it. She rose
to bundle herself back up for the winter air.
"I don't mean to be a bother. I —" She stopped
as Ernest suddenly backed away. He saw her face.
He didn't know her at all. *Of course we are the same
and all alike to them,* she thought. And then he did
the thing with his nose, that testing-the-air twitch
to see if you smelled funny. No matter
that Charles always told her no lady
had ever smelled so nice as when
she morning'd him with her rosy air.

"I'll get in trouble if the pastor sees.
You'd better go down and out the back, now."
He pointed. He looked at his watch.
His teeth looked to chatter squirrel-like.
"I'll be on my way, Mr. Ernest,"
she answered him. "Just let me give
a nod to the Lord, and I'll not trouble you."
Before he could protest she reached the altar-rail,
looked up in awe at how the morning light halo'd
the sad Christ, while red-glow dabbles
daubed his wounds and nails that put them
in hell-light. He may have fed five thousand,
but a house and a warm bed were something else.

ii
She had to walk slowly. Loucks Avenue
was piled with snow. One narrow way
had been shoveled and tramped to some
resemblance to a foot-path. Somewhere beneath
the hillocks of snow were peoples' cars.
Her shoes slid this-way, that-way; she tumbled
sideways more than once until Broadway
where she could walk the roadway.
Few cars were out, and let them make way
for her instead of she for them. She was
seventy, and seventy should have at least
the right of way on a Sunday morning.

Nothing was warming up. Trees groaned
as they tried to gird themselves in
against the killing cold. Her thoughts
in the mile she'd have to walk, were on
the sun that would soon pain her eyes
as it slid its low path into noon-time.
That sun might warm her house a little,
she reasoned. And there was one last plan
to get her through the cold spell. But first
she had to tread the long walk of mill-fence —
nothing shoveled, no path except the road —
along the smoky factory that made long tubes
of shiny metal that filled the rail-cars, day
and night of pounding and grinding, lights
on and off at all hours. Coal, coke
and the working of the earth's metals were all
that this town was about. Charles had worked,
until the black lung killed him, one mine
and then another and another, always
the parts of the mines the white men avoided.
Charlie and the Negro gang worked side
by side with a bunch of Hungarians, almost
as much despised for their one-off language,
their dark-eyed pride and intransigence.
Just to defy and baffle their bosses,
some of the Negro miners learned "Hunky talk,"

enough to joke and drink together, enough
to be able to fool the foreman and warn each other
when something too dangerous was asked for.
She went along. The Hunky women didn't like it
when she learned a few words on her own
and Charlie and the Kovacs and she
would laugh and pass a bottle amongst them.
But that was before ...

iii
Over the bridge and past Caruso's, the store
that gave her credit and saved her more
times than she could count, then up the hill
to her own steep-stepped house she went.
In through the unlocked door, into the kitchen.
Lightless, heatless, her breath went icy
the moment she got inside. It was colder here,
for she had covered up the window so wind
would not get in, but neither did the sunlight.
No matter. She had her plan, the one
that came to her just as she awakened.
She only needed a little coal. The furnace, dead,
would never come to life until a truck came,
filling the chute below with welcome fuel.
But the coal stove would do, and huddled near
she could get through the day. Tomorrow's mail
might bring the cash that LeRoi sent
each month from his pay in far-off Korea.

This was pride swallowed, her pride of home
and of needing nothing, ever, 'cept what folks paid
when she helped them out, or sewed, or watched
a baby that needed minding. Now she, Cora,
would beg from door to door. The neighbors
would hear her bowed voice a-tremble and ask
for just a bucket or two of coal. That's all.

She lifted the bucket. She opened the door.
Five houses this side of Kingview Road, five
on the other side. That ought to do it.
They must all be home. Smoke rose black
from every chimney. It wasn't as though
she was really begging: the *loan* of some coal
was all she would ask, and then she'd pay
it back when the delivery came. That's all.

Knocked on one door. They yelled inside,
argued on who should answer her knocking.
Man's voice bellowing, woman in turn.
Two lions in a cage would have been quieter.
She knocked again. Lace curtain parted.
Two eyes regarded her from shadowed parlor.
Then from behind those eyes, the man
called out, "Get off our steps! Go on!
Whatever you're selling or preaching,
just go away!" She turned and sighed.

At the Polish neighbors' home, despite
the puffing chimney, there was no answer.
They went to Mass early, she remembered.
They would be back, confession-clean,
but not for hours to come. She tried
another door, the old widower's, but no,
he didn't answer, either. The bottles piled
along the porch floor told a dead-drunk tale.
He might not rouse himself till after noon.

Her feet gone numb again, she knocked
at the Kovak house. Charlie had worked
with their father until the explosion
made Mrs. Kovak a widow, her sons
into angry orphans always in trouble.
Now Cora smiled as someone came running
for she had a way in mind to reach out
to the reclusive and suspicious widow.

It was the younger boy who answered.
He had just got out of bed; his hair
was awry in every direction; he rubbed
his eyes and tried to make out her face.

"What d'ye want," he asked her angrily. —
"Let me talk to your mother, please."
He shrugged and walked away. She waited
and felt the rush of warm air from the open
doorway. The disheveled mother came.
She spoke almost no English, after all these years!
"*Mit akarsz?*" she demanded, closing the door
so only her head and shoulders stuck out. —
"I am your neighbor, Mrs. Kovac." She paused,
then sorting her memory of the old days,
"*Szomszéd.* Neighbor." — The woman started.
"Mit akarsz?" she asked again. *What do you want?* —
"I am Charlie's wife. *Charles felesége. Szomszéd.*" —
The woman held out her hands in consternation.
Cora raised the empty bucket. "I need some coal.
Van … szén?" — Then Mrs. Kovac backed away.

The door got wide again. An older boy
came up behind her. He had a stick.
He slapped it against his open palm. "Some coal.
Van … szén?" Had she forgotten everything?
    What word
would make her message clear except,
   "Please, please?"
There it was: the word, *kérem.* "*Kérem. Van szén?*"

The door slammed shut. At five more houses,
there was no one present, or everyone pretended
to be somewhere else, intent on television.

iv
Cora sat in the kitchen. She wrapped herself
in a blanket, tied rags around her feet to keep
the frost at bay. She'd seen a movie once
where they broke up the furniture to feed a stove,
but she didn't know how to do that. Two hands,
at seventy, frost-bitten and without a hammer,
what could she do? Would the neighbors talk?
Would they come around at last when they realized
she was there alone with no light or stove or coal?
Did the Methodist Episcopal Jesus care?

v
I was ten years old when the police came,
and then an ambulance, and there she was
on a stretcher, the bundled-up frozen woman.
The door had blown open; the mailman found her.
Neighbors flowed out of their homes like wax
atop a fast-melting candle. All bundled up
against the cold wave, the word balloons
above all their comic-book faces repeated:
She froze to death. She froze to death.
      She froze to death.

One voice opined, "How could this happen here,
right in our midst, right on our street?"
"She was too proud to ask for help,"
      someone else offered.
The new word-balloon passed among them.
It was taken up as an anthem, *too proud, too proud
to ask for help, of course we would have helped.
Too proud, too proud to ask for help.*
And then the little Hungarian boy called out,
"But there was a Negro lady asking for coal.
I saw her. A Negro lady asking —"

A hand reached out and covered his mouth.
The crowd went on murmuring
    until the ambulance was gone.
As the last door to the last house closed
the word-balloon lingered, one cloud
over all the chimneys, lettering
She froze to death.
              She froze to death.
                            She froze —

OLD SCHOLAR UNDER AUTUMN TREES (ANNIVERSARIUS XLVIII)

*From a Chinese Painting
and Poem by Shen Zhou, 1470 CE.*

Gone, gone, gone. Gone to the west
wind, the leaves have fled. Still, there is
sun, still some shade under half-
disrobed maples. I loosen
my collar, I just lean back
and read my book. No clock, no
appointments, all idleness.
It is a long book; I have
all the Autumn ahead
to read, or to gaze on up
at the sky that pulls on me.
Here below — or on up there —
who knows what I shall do next?

— *January 19, 2020, from a 2006 journal.*

THE MAN WHO HATED TREES

Stake through its heart, the sap-bled
tree grew ashen. Leafless, barkless,
squirrel-shunned, at last it was
    patently dead.
My Bonn Place neighbors wondered
  what manner of deviant
  could so impale
one of our dwindling row of sycamores,
our whispering rain-umbrellas,
our sparrow and robin high-rise
  low-income condominiums.
What manner of deviant
  to saw the branches last fall,
  then, angered at twig-break
  through this spring's bark —
    the insouciant sucker growth
    attempting new sun-search —
to drive that railroad spike
into heartwood, cutting the xylem
and phloem course from roots
to yearning bud?
Did he snap those twigs off, too?
Does he harbor a death-wish
  for all of our loved trees?
One morning in summer the scream
  of chainsaw awakens us.
Two dog-ladies discover the amputee
  slices of trunk on the lawn,
stacked for the trash man,
  ham-steaks of tree-trunk.
We gather,
  hold hands,
    and count the rings.

          — Found in a notebook from c. 1975,
                          Weehawken, NJ.

THE HEADLESS CROSS AT ELSDON

after a dirge by Robert Surtees

Her lover died at the Nine-Stone Rig
from seven brothers' rage;
nine the arrows that shower'd down,
arms, heart, and throat, and eye

a-shiver with the hate-fletched shafts,
a-quake with their envenom'd darts,
a double death of blood and poison,
all this to avenge a virginity lost!

They shot him dead at the Nine-Stone Rig,
beside the cursèd cross of Thor
(false Dane who absolution shunned),
a fitting place to die.

They left him lying in his blood,
red on green moss, black on brown earth.
They fled and vowed to kill again
if her illicit union spawn'd.

A Lapland wind, a raven dark,
lapped at the blood and plucked the eye,
the one blue orb unarrow'd,
and brought it to the lady fair.

She fainted, for she knew that eye,
beneath which she had loved and sigh'd.
And then she summon'd her menials
to search the wet, cold ground for him.

They made a bier from broken boughs
of the birch and the aspen gray.
Nine arrows they broke and cast away
at the foot of the Headless Cross.

They bore him to Our Lady's Chapel.
None dared to refuse his passing-in.
The lady arrived. Her servant brought,
in a silver chalice, the azure eye.

She placed the ball in the blacken'd hole
where once it had glistened and tear'd.
The other had but the stump of wood
where the unkindest dart of all

had blinded him, and reft her soul.
They waked him there all day; by night
the tapers burned as monks and nuns
gave out heart-rending Requiems.

As they came as last to bear him off,
the lady threw her robes aside,
in favor of an ashen shift, sleev'd
and collar'd with crimson and black.

With waters blessed from Our Lady's well,
she bathed the corpse, and washed it clean
of the thrice-three poison'd wounds.
(Her wound only did she not regret).

She plaited a garland for on his breast,
and a garland for on his hair.
The raven upon her shoulder lit.
The Lapland wind made dark the room

as the tapers all flickered and died.
They rolled him in a winding sheet
    ah, lily-white it was! And as
the Virgin's water had him blessed,

no mark of blood appeared.
They bore him to a new-made grave,
and passing by the Chapel Garth
they paused to let the Gray Friars sing

in yet another Requiem. But where
would the lady bury her lover?
Not in the family crypt where bones
might still be ravaged by those

same seven brothers she now loathed!
Not in some crowded churchy ground
where twenty years hence they'd dig
and pile his bones with strangers' skulls!

She chose the place, in dark of wood
where first they had met, o fatal spot!
a bower beneath a spreading beech.

In murk of midnight they buried him,
where the dew fell cold and still,
in windless fell of untrembling leaf
where the mists cling to the hill.

They dug his grave just a bare foot deep,
where she had happily lain with him:
see where the heather flower blooms,
and the moss and the lady-fern.

A Gray Friar stood upon that grave
and sang until the sun rose true,
and another sings for the lover's soul
in the shade of the Headless Cross.

ODE 2: THE THUNDERSTORM, 1968

We are alone, in slum-student-
house apartment, windows agape
into a rainstorm,
hot summer viewed as multiples
through fly-eyed screens, each eye-spread
alike intoning solitude, pinpoints of night,
scattered and re-assembled.

Impossibilities abroad,
walk on the howling wind,
invisibly strut
between the streetlight cycles,
translate through mesh as spectral whirl,
their passing marked by sourceless rings
spun out on pools of rain.

Across the square,
someone else's windows
spill out blackness,
a tumbling emptiness
where lights had been.
Have they gone to sleep
or do they reach for one
another over there, in
blundering lust? Does someone
over there moan, "Please!"
and the other cry, "Yes"?

Or does another solitude therein,
sigh and partake
of yearning night? For after all,
what is a storm but electrical
attraction gone mad? Most
creatures hide from a tempest,
and he who hides, trembles
alone in the dark.
Two in an arm-chair,

we lean and look
at the gaping empty
mouths of storefronts,
a neon flicker, failing,
from the Hotel Bar.

High-minded, we
ridicule the passions,
pretending my hand that touches your arm
is not and does not what it seems
but is a mere acting-out
of the diamond-spun
songs from a phonograph.

I share
the singer's illusion, loss, and hope,
the stuff of blues and Broadway.
The songs are never true; they are
always and ever about the thing
you want, but cannot have.

I on the verge of dangerous descent,
gulp in a breath of cynic air,
but what I draw, what sifts
through the wind-tattered
screen, belies the song,
is love.

Later, I find you, already asleep
(or feigning sleep), the half-bed
moon-dark inviting me.
I hold you, warmed by your heat,
blessed by my storm-wrought hope,

while in the next room
two lovers sweat obliviously.
(They have abandoned themselves,
but neither you nor I can
surrender to this moment.)

So I, poised where our bodies touch
lay dreamless, feeling you breathe,
you, in wanting and terror, feel
my breath and pulse and desire.

Dawn finds me at the lakeside bench
accusing the sun and sparrow flight
for ending my happiness.
You were still sleeping; perhaps
you only think you dreamt of me.
If only your dreaming self
could wed my waking madness!

— Edinboro, PA, 1968, Revised February 2020.

Photo by Tony Buba.

THE MATTRESS, VERTICAL

after a photo by Tony Buba

The mattress, vertical,
sleeps none.
Humans and dogs
and cats, flakes
of dry skin and dust mites,
a slurry of cracker crumbs
and the sighs of forgotten
orgasms, have sloughed away
into the hungry soil
of the abandoned weedlot.

The mattress, vertical,
more like a tombstone
than a nuptial platform,
dimpled with stitching,
dappled with silhouette
of starving treescape,
is hungry for occupants,
makes do with shadows —

a traffic cone considers
a rest, inscribes a "V,"
then an inverted signature,
as if to stake a claim.
The photographer, retired,
just comes up short
of putting his outline there.
He hesitates; he's nearly
always sleepy this time of day.
One step forward, one
step back, he pauses.

No one would notice
if he reclined a while,
just thirty minutes until he'd
be as good as new. But no:
the thought of bedbugs,
hands reaching for his camera,
the curiosity of skunk and badger.

Better to let
a mattress, vertical
go on about
its very important business.
Whatever that is.

THE NIGHT I ALMOST FLEW

By water's edge
I tramp compliant grass
into a dancing ring,
sing on the breeze a name
no mouth has uttered here
since the white man came.

In earthward turn of wrist
I thrust an airless wing
against a blast
if the idea of uplift.

In flex of arm, I seem to rise
into the memory of flight —
I have been here before
in childhood levitation,
hand on banister, yet feet
not touching any but the top
and bottom stair-tread —

Blocked at the last by weight,
I sink! The weight of *what?*
Cloth, shoes, a belt, a watch,
the fear of spectacles
dashed onto the rocks below
should I rise too far and fast.

Must one be naked for this?
To become weightless
is no small matter!

— 1974/ rev 2020

THEY CLOSED HIS EYES

after Gustavo Adolfo Bécquer

I went to visit a dying friend,
for one last time. His eyes
were open. I took his bony hand
and pressed it. His fingers clutched
at life, and he gasped a name
(not mine) and said, "I always
loved you best of all." I lied,
and said I loved him equally.

No mother, brother, lover, son,
no sister, cousin or father
came to stand by as the tubes
were removed, the machine
silenced and wheeled away.

They closed his eyes
that were open still
and wanted to be open
still for the coming sunrise,
mirror-red on the East River.
They hid his face
with a white linen.

And out of nowhere
anonymous mourners came,
some sobbing, some silent.
They come each day, I am told,
and they come for everyone
who has no one. They stood
as the bed frame was dropped
and the wheeled death-cart
was moved to its side.
From the sad sickroom,
they moved away like shadows
and vanished in the corridor.

In a dish, the night candle
burned on a low table.
It cast on the wall
the deathbed's outline,
and in that shadow
the sharp lines
of his wasted body.
The dawn appeared
pearl white and then ruby red.
With a thousand noises
the city exploded to life:
horns, sirens, jackhammers
and the mournful hum
of traffic far below.
As ordinary light
cascaded into the death-room,
I thought for a moment:

*How much more lonely than we
are the newly-dead!*

On the shoulders of men
who did not know his name,
gloved and face-masked
against the feared contagion
they bore him away
and in a chapel left
the freshly-wrapped body
on a plywood bier.
A number was stenciled there.
Then others surrounded
his pale body
with yellow candles
and things of black crèpe,
disposable grief that had
no shape but the wing-edge
of a dusty raven, no use
except to fill the space
between the corpse
and the imaginary public.

No one came. Well, almost
no one: a bag lady crone
put down her burden and knelt,
mumbled some prayers
and shuffled off. She crossed
the narrow nave. Door moaned,
opened without a hand
upon it to let her out.
The holy place was quiet,
a cell of silence as a barrage
of taxi hails and basketball
court echoes filtered in
through a broken window.
One pigeon fluttered in,
cooed disapproving
that it was not a rice-wedding,
then flapped away.

I was directed there.
Some hours had passed.
I stood alone, or nearly so.
A young priest approached,
saw who and what was there
to be blessed and buried,
covered his face,
and hurried away.
My ears reached out
until I could hear
the chapel's one clock
in measured ticking.
A bank of candles
to one side of the nave
took to guttering
at the same beat
as my own breathing.

All things here
were so dark and mournful,
rigid and cold,
not even a tear was welcome,
and I thought for a moment:

*How much more lonely than we
are the newly-dead!*

Should there not be
a legion of mourners?
Should he not be
where all who knew him
could gather and mourn?
I imagine the high belfry
of his New England town,
the iron tongue clanging
of the funeral bells,
mournful in last farewell.
Veils and black suits,
eyes cast down in grief,
his friends and relatives
passed in a line and shook
each other's hands, and hugged.

And in that high place
in the old family's last vault,
dark and narrow,
crowded with his ancestors,
the crowbar opened
a niche at one end,
and they laid him away there,
then sealed it up
amid a hecatomb of camellias.
Newspapers would show
the memorial plaque;
friends would come annually.

But this was not to be.
New England paid no dues
to a death in New York,
a death of *that* kind among
those kinds of people.

The body, on its plywood
plinth, would go instead
into a plywood casket,
then onto a barge,
with hundreds of like kind,
piled high and hauled across
to the Potter's Field
on desolate Hart Island.

Pick-axe on shoulder,
the convict gravedigger,
cursing his lot in dawn-fog,
stood on a mound. His box,
among many other
numbered boxes, dropped
into a numbered plot.
Not a word was said,
not even a prayer.

It was silent. Only now,
after years of dream-dread
can I see it: headlong,
crooked, piled one
upon another at crazy angles,
a quilt of coffins, at last
death's final suffocation
into a nameless grave.
And I sit up in my bed
and think:

*How much more lonely than we
are the unmarked dead!*

On winter nights
in bitter darkness,
when wind makes
the rafters chatter,
when whipped rain
lashes the window panes,
in such a lonely time
I remember my poor friend,
and the nameless dead
heaped up with him:
how many had I touched?
how many had touched me?

There on Hart Island,
in the pit full of brother-souls,
do they hear the rain
with its same yet ever-
changing monody?
Do they hear the winds'
stern fights across the bay,
the tug boats, the fog-horns,
the sway-song of tides buoyed
by the revolving moon?
Do their bones freeze
with the cold of winter?

Does dust to dust return?
Do souls abandoned by earth
have any place in any heaven?
Or is it all the rot of matter,
organic filthiness and worms?
I do not know. I tramp most
graveyards merrily. I am not
a morose or gloomy soul, and yet,
something there is — something
that treads behind my nights
with loathing and terror.

City of a billion lights, city
of symphonies and towers
aspiring to Promethean heights:
how did a hundred thousand souls
perish in your averted gaze?
A hundred thousand brother-dead
I cannot begin to mourn and cannot
even count.

*How much more lonely than we
are the hundred thousand dead
who have gone on without us?*

Gustavo Adolfo Bécquer (1836-1870), a Spanish poet from Seville, influenced by E.T.A Hoffmann and Heinrich Heine, wrote an elegiac poem titled "They Closed Her Eyes." I have gender-changed, "written over," and expanded upon his poem for this work, which is in memory of the 100,000 fatalities from HIV in New York during the 1980s, specifically those who wound up in the Potter's Field because no family would claim their bodies.

HE WAS NOT THERE, HE IS NOT HERE

In memoriam Kleber de Freitas

The frog, foot-pads pressed
against the laundry-room
window croaks, "*Where is he?
Where is he?*" But there is
no answer.

The dragonfly buzz-hovers
majestically, striped
like a Brazilian flag,
floats at the center
of your vision,
persistent-questioning:
Onde ele esta? Onde ele esta?

The fox Renard, head bent
to sip at garden pond,
darts into darkness, tail
red and bushy waving
a question mark:
Wo ist er? Wo ist er?

Two birds, one
nightingale, one
lark, keep vigil,
songs just at dawn
for a moment entwined:
"*Où est-il? Où est-il?*"

Last night a star-scarf,
a shimmering nebula
of Orionids, flew from the roof
to the rustic cemetery,
a Siberian breeze
chill-sighing "*Gdye on? Gdye on?*"

The grave-ground sleeps,
awaiting its permanent marker.
A poet murmurs,
Where art thou? Where art thou?

Fear not: the Faun has flown.
He was not there; he is not here.
He has leaped the ravine,
long legs striding
the opposite tree-line,
the arc of the nymph-scarf
of Isadora, draped
on the branches
leads him on,
as does an orchestra of crickets.
He bounds wild-free in oak and maple
grand jeté beneath a canopy
of rampant stars.

FROM THE LIPS OF THE LAST INCA

freely adapted from a poem by José Eusebio Caro (1817-1853)

I left the white men far behind —
in vain they search the canyon's deep.
Today I have scaled Pichincha's rim.
I pace its edge as the sun does,
wandering, passionate, and free.

Much'aykusqayki, Tayta Inti!
Hail, Father Sun! Though Manco's throne,
the nearest seat on earth to your
flaming presence, lies in the dust,
though everywhere your sacred altars
groan profaned, I come alone, but free.

Much'aykusqayki, Tayta Inti!
Hail, Father Sun! No brand or chain
makes me a slave of any nation.
No white man shall boast he killed me —
I kill myself, and free I die!

Sun, when you begin to sink, this
volcano will burn and hold me.
Regard me from the distant sea
as I walk downward, resolute,
singing your hymns to lava's brink.

Tomorrow, raying forth, your crown
will shine anew on the east slope,
and then at your blazing noon-time
your rays shall gild my new ashes:
some bones, some scattered beads of me,
glint of a gold armband, my bow
and ten consecrated arrows.
O Pichincha, hearth of freedom!

Much'aykusqayki, Mallku Kuntur!
Hail, King of the Condors, come down
and make this summit your palace.
There will be scant of me to feed you,
but on my soft ash take respite,
for mate and nest and eggs anew.
And I, King of Nothing, unknown,
shall with you fly, invisible,
nameless forever, and forever free.

José Eusebio Caro (1817-1853) lived in New Granada (present-day Colombia), and was co-founder of his nation's first literary journal, *Le Estrella National* in 1836. I have added salutations in Quechua, the language of the Incas, which were not in the original poem.

Regarding the volcano named Pichincha, which is in Ecuador, *Wikipedia* notes, "On May 24, 1822, General Sucre's southern campaign in the Spanish–American War of independence came to a climax when his forces defeated the Spanish colonial army on the southeast slopes of this volcano. The engagement, known as the Battle of Pichincha, secured the independence of the territories of present-day Ecuador."

NOCTURNE III

Adapted from a poem by José Asuncion Silva (1865-1896)

On such a night — how shall I describe it? —
A night all full of murmurings, of the brush
of invisible wings, of perfumes indefinable,
a night within whose glooms of vague forest,
fireflies went on and off sepulchrally —
or was it a nuptial flickering that led us on? —
as meekly you accompanied me, silent,
slender, hushed, and pale, as though such thoughts,
such double presentiments of joy and doom
troubled the very depths of your soul, too.
Glow-worms and the night-ghosted asphodels
spelled out our distant path across the plain.
One sandaled foot before the other tread,
you walked with me, and the spherical moon,
bloated in heaven's serge and indigo,
shed light, a beacon out of infinity.

Your shadow, so delicate and languid,
and my shadow, graven by white lunar light
upon the sands of the path before us,
were joined together
deep umbra as one, indefinite shades
of edged penumbra, joined as one,
two as one in a great, single shadow,
two as one in a great, single shadow,
two as one in a great, single shadow.

Gone is that night! Gone! But now another,
solitary, choked full of infinite
woes and the sharp agony of mourning,
on the same path as then, still and lonely
I came — why here again on such a night? —

parted from you by the passing of time,
by the door of your tomb, by arguments
unreconciled, the leaden density
which neither your voice nor mine pierced through.
Still and lonely — why here again at night?

And the hounds of the wood (or were they wolves?)
bayed at the moon (did they not care for it,
this moon of pale visage, bloodless?)
Were they not troubled, as I was,
by the frogs' croak at the bottomless mere?

Cold came and pierced me to shuddering,
cold such as the chill that on your bed
stole color from your cheeks and neck and hands,
the chill in its snowy whiteness, the white
of the winding sheet, the bleached shroud.
It was the cold of mausoleum air,
it was the chill of the advancing tread
of Death, the unwanted frost of shut eyes.

And my shadow, graven by white lunar light,
went on the path alone,
went on the path alone,
not calling out your name (I have no right!),
went on the path to the wastes of solitude.

But then your shadow, so delicate and languid,
slender, hushed, and pale, as on that night
of your dying on the first moon of Spring,
as on that night all full of murmurings,
of the brush of wings, of perfumes indefinable,
came up close by and walked with me,
came up close by and walked with me,
came up close by and walked with me —
my shadow with its black umbra,
my shadow with its vaguely-edged penumbra
(yours the fluttering edge of penumbra only,
O shadow without a living source!)

two as one joined in a great, single shadow,
two as one joined in a great, single shadow.
Oh, shadows of the living and of the dead, joined
as one, two shadows running
each to the other in nights of woe and tears!

"Nocturne" was written in 1892 by Colombian poet José Asuncion Silva. He had lived in Europe and knew Mallarmé and other leading French poets. His poetry is a precursor of modernism in Latin American poetry, and, in this one in particular, he inhabits the world and esthetics of Poe's poems. Suggestive of "Ulalume," hypnotic with its repetition and its shadowy images, this poem was also doubtless provoked by the death of his beloved sister in the same year. Three years later, all the poet's unpublished works were lost in a shipwreck. A year after that, Silva committed suicide.

"Nocturne," written in free verse, defied the classical, formal mode of most poetry in Spanish.

In this adaptation I have made the supernatural suggestiveness of the poem stronger – it is not possible to work on a piece such as this without being completely overshadowed by "Ulalume." I have also introduced the concept of the double-shadow: the umbra is the dark, solid part of a shadow, and the penumbra is a shadow's vague, poorly-defined edges. Silva does not employ these terms, so this is my addition. I have also removed the gender of the dead loved one, because, well, that is what I do. Silva repeats lines almost with a hypnotic intent, so I have done the same in my version, also permitting some exact phrases from the opening of the poem to find their way in again near the end, like a musical reprise.

It is simultaneously, a very Gothic poem, and a very modern poem. It is one of the most important Spanish-language poems I have engaged with.

GUESTS AT OUR COUNTRY PLACE

Apocalypse impending,
guests flock
to our country home.

The visiting Surrealist painter
arranged our furniture
at impossible angles,
then signed his name
on our ceiling.
When you sell,
he assures us,
you can name your price.

The visiting poet,
eats but doesn't write,
burns up the last
of our emergency
candles for inspiration.
As hint we put
his suitcase at the door.
He moves it back.
The guest room smells
of ganja
and burnt paper.

The visiting English prof
found the cream sherry,
the Riesling wine.
The tab so far:
empty bottles,
green-stemmed Rhine glasses
toppled and broken;
our daughter
seduced.

This being a rural town
we can call the police
from a remote location
to report a trespass.

The resulting raid
with paramilitary gear
will clear the lot out,
since sheriffs now
come in shooting
and sort out who
at the county morgue.

THE SECRET

Since you had to leave town, I lived
in West Newton with "Gertrude and Claudius."
The town hugged two river banks
of the angry, dark Youghiogheny. Hornets
buzzed on the bridge that divided it.
Trains roared through the middle
of the tiny main street. It was a place
you went when you needed to be
where no one knew your original name
or why you left where you came from,
where a man and a woman could pretend
to be married, and no one asked
for proof on paper. So I was Hamlet,
in teen-boy guise, housed with my mother
and the man who was once an uncle,
now a no-name lord of the manor.
In my basement laboratory I tried
in vain to make alchemical potions
that might turn a grown man to a frog,
or tastelessly poison a chutney jar.
None of my called-down curses ever worked.
The miscreant sat in his TV room at night
watching *Gunsmoke* and John Wayne westerns.
My mother spawned a daughter, and then
a son as well, while "Uncle" spewed scorn
on my useless, book-centered universe.
He railed against Jews, bragged that the town
would never build a park or a swimming pool
"'cause if we did, the niggers would come."

He made me know I was not welcome,
a bookworm boarder to last as long
as the child support payments came
from my silent and absent father,
and after that, "I want you gone."

The house had one book only
that was not mine: on the dryer,
opposite their bedroom door,
a well-leafed copy of *Lady Chatterley's
Lover* that opened instantly
to the sex scenes. My uncle
had used it to seduce my mother,
sweet poison to eye and ear.

I tried to imagine their coupling,
but judging from the contents
of the medicine cabinet, for
hemorrhoids, psoriasis, and
unpronounceable ailments, all
I could picture was something
like a Hammer Films blob
undulating upon a mattress,
as though two pizza slices
had toppled upon one another
inside the melting oven.

Late afternoons, she went
to the bar at the Moose Club.
He went there straight from work.
They came home brawling drunk
when the bar ejected them.
I cooked the dinners,
changed the diapers,
stood guard at Elsinore's
rotting clapboards.

Finally I maneuvered out
of these weekday horrors:
I stayed at school as late as I could,
volunteered for anything that kept
my presence from his shadow.

The new town
tolerated me. I had Latin at last
to occupy my thoughts,
new streets to haunt,
a vast night gallery
of riverside graves
where I could brood
and plan my escape
or some spectacular
suicide.

When poetry came,
I figured I wouldn't last
to thirty, anyway.

When summer arrived
and I could run off
to my grandmother's house,
"out home," a scant five miles
from Scottdale,
the exultation of home
came back to me.

I phoned my friends in town,
and one by one their mothers
answered and said, "No,
Tim's not around." "Dave
won't be around this summer."
"Tom is not permitted
to take a phone call right now."
I never saw my friends again.

Decades — no, a lifetime later,
I hear from an old neighbor,
the Polish girl whose porch
we could see from our kitchen
window. "You were just gone,"
she told me. "One day, just gone.

Our parents wouldn't tell us why.
Your whole family just vanished,
gone without a word."

I choked up as she told me,
"We cried forever."

And why, and what
was so unspeakable:
My mother took up
with my father's sister's husband,
and not content to run away,
they wove a story:
that my father and his sister
"did it first." Incest, that is.
Their proof: a missing condom
that his young daughter and a friend
had blown up as a water balloon
and thrown away in secret;
and the mailman's account
of seeing someone naked
moving around in the afternoon,
pale skin viewed through panes
of a curtained inner doorway.

So, armed with "They did it first,"
and D. H. Lawrence, the furtive nights
and parked-car couplings began.
Two divorces, and the flood
of door-to-door and phone-
to-phone gossiping. *Have you heard
about the Rutherford incest?
Brother and sister — the mailman saw
everything. And wasn't it almost
incest, what the other two did,
a woman and her in-law?*

More than four decades later,
when I came to the town again, the street
of yellow bricks greeted me
with a full rainbow against
the backdrop of nearby hills.
It was just a town. A place
of stately homes, a new library,
a red brick church
my great-grandparents helped build.

I ought to feel happy here.
The graves of my ancestors
are here in their fine plots.
My grandfather had been Burgess,
a great-uncle a financier;
the Rutherford building
neck-to-neck with Frick,
even a Rutherford bookstore once.

Yet I kept looking backwards,
tense at each corner, expecting
the crowd with pitchforks,
torches hastily lit to be rid of me.

Who can undo
the evil of false witnessing?

Who can come home
to where they "cried forever?"

THE F- - - POEM

Word I won't say,
Word I won't write,
Word I wince
to listen to,
and pity the speaker
for ignorance
and verbal incontinence,

word that should make
even a peasant blush.
Films laced with it
I leave, postings and memes
I hide from all view.

Citizens:
how will peace come
when f—
is your mantra?

Will blessings come
by invoking
Mother F—
day in and out?

I am glad to know
that Shakespeare did not
put an f—
into the mouth
of a single actor.

Strange to think
that so much depends
not on inspirations,
compulsions, labor
for love, or for the sake
of a red wheelbarrow.

Instead, the whip
that keeps them going
is the endless flashback
to penetration:

active, passive,
past, present,
subjunctive,
imperative,

F— on,
F— off,
like breath
or a heartbeat.

Why not just name
the whole planet F—
and be done with it?

BEING TOO MUCH WITH THE STARS

translation of an untitled poem by
José Asunción Silva (1865-1896)

Stars range between
the gloom of obscurity
and sheer immensity,
some like pale wisps
of incense in a vacuum.
Nebulae, you burn so far
into infinity it frightens me;
that all that reaches earth
is but your light reflected;
suns fallen, gone
into an unknown abyss
shedding an unknown radiance;
constellations — mirages
the magicians once worshiped;
millions of distant planets,
flowers in a fantastic brooch,
clear islands afloat in night,
a sea without end or bottom.
Burning stars, far pensive lights,
dim eyes with wavering pupils —
Burning stars! Why are you silent,
if you live, and why do you shine
if you are already dead?

Estrellas que entre lo sombrío
de lo ignorado y de lo inmenso,
asemejáis en el vacío
jirones pálidos de incienso;
nebulosas que ardéis tan lejos
en el infinito que aterra,
que sólo alcanzan los reflejos
de vuestra luz hasta la tierra;
astros que en abismos ignotos
derramáis resplandores vagos,
constelaciones que en remotos
tiempos adoraron los magos;
millones de mundos lejanos,
flores de fantástico broche,
islas claras en los océanos
sin fin ni fondo de la noche;
¡Estrellas, luces pensativas!
¡Estrellas, pupilas inciertas!
¿Por qué os calláis si estáis vivas,
y por qué alumbráis si estáis muertas?

— *José Asunción Silva*

IN THE MIST

I have grown into
my solitude,
the cloud
of not seeing;
the echo back
of my own voice
assures me of what
is beyond the veil
of viral fog.

O visitors, visitors!
A social interdict
lies between us.
Men came one night
(handsome criminals!).
They rifled through
everything, my honor
more injured than anything.
Some silverware
has gone missing,
a toppled clock,
an antique
barometer gone
to some pawn shop.

I gave them only
slight amusement,
the last dregs
of old green tea,
the savor
of lime marmalade,
dry rolls
from the cold oven.

The leavings of little
cigarettes
on the winding stairs,
the violated door
that will no longer close
entirely — my penalties.

I am fine.
I sleep without locks.
No one comes.
My voice has a certain
monotony; my poems
say, *stay away,*
stay away.

And who am I?
Only a lighthouse,
my voice
the foghorn's
dismal
utterance.

MOONLIGHT IN THE CEMETERY

*Adapted from Théophile Gautier's
"Au Cimitière: Claire de Lune"*

That white tomb — do you know the one
and whose it is? — where in the yew's shade
there floats a plaintive sound?
Upon the yew, always the same pale dove
lonely and sad at each sun's setting
utters his night-long threnody:

an aria tenderly morbid,
as charming as it is fatal,
a song that gives you pain
yet which you long to hear forever;
an air like the other-worldly sigh
of a love-sick angel.

One imagines the dead soul wakes
to weep down there in unison
with the forlorn lament, and in the misery
of being forgotten, it too complains
as soft and sweet as dove-song.

On the wings of this melody
all kinds of recollections return.
Whose shade is that? What form
angelic hovers in a beam of light?
O veil of whiteness! Yet linger not,

beware the night-bloom beauty,
closing and opening, rich
in hypnotic scent around you; beware,
in yew-shade cast in moonlight
upon that white tomb inescapable
the phantom's outstretched arms,

the gesture vaguely beckoning,
and just as vaguely warning you away,
the almost inaudible murmuring:
*Flee now! But will you not
come back again in moonlight?*

O never again when night
drops its black mantle
upon the yew, the tomb,
and the obsessive-singing
dove who its its captive, never
shall I return to hear
that plaintive, mourning song!

**Au Cimetière: Claire de lune.
Théophile Gautier (1811-1872)**

Connaissez-vous la blanche tombe,
Où flotte avec un son plaintif
L'ombre d'un if?
Sur l'if une pâle colombe,
Triste et seule, au soleil couchant,
Chante son chant:

Un air maladivement tendre,
À la fois charmant et fatal,
Qui vous fait mal,
Et qu'on voudrait toujours entendre;
Un air, comme en soupire aux cieux
L'ange amoureux.

On dirait que l'âme éveillée
Pleure sous terre; à l'unisson
De la chanson,
Et, du malheur d'être oubliée
Se plaint dans un roucoulement
Bien doucement.
    Sur les ailes de la musique

On sent lentement revenir
Un souvenir;
Une ombre de forme angélique,
Passe dans un rayon tremblant,
En voile blanc.

Les belles-de-nuit demi-closes,
Jettent leur parfum faible et doux
Autour de vous,
Et le fantôme aux molles poses
Murmure en vous tendant les bras:
Tu reviendras!

Oh! jamais plus, près de la tombe,
Je n'irai, quand descend le soir
Au manteau noir,
Écouter la pâle colombe
Chanter, sur la branche de l'if
Son chant plaintif!

THE OVERNIGHT ANGEL

He followed me home.
He stayed the night.
He left the next morning.

He knows, and I know,
that I will never see him again.
He did everything I wanted.
One time.

If angels are
those radiant ones
who love us unbidden
and justify the ways
of Love
to Solitude,
I know what angels are.

— Jan 1982, rev. 2020

BECOMING INVISIBLE

The price I pay for my poems:
I filter light and air, make
verse of phosphorescent hopes.
From paleness I progress
to full transparency.

I am invisible. Doors close
in my face with no one to hold
them open, feet stamp on mine,
elbows and briefcases jab me.
If I wave, no taxi stops,
or if it stops, another jostles in
to the seat that should have been mine.
Crowds pass me by
without a blink or nod.
Beauty becomes unbearable
to see, now that it's blind
to me. That I, its priest
and celebrant, should be
disbarred!

I leave my poems
where you might find them.
I wait at your kitchen table,
not offered tea, as you read
the newspaper, frown-puzzle
over the Sunday crossword,
then tip my manuscript
into the trash with grocer's ads
and mail-order catalogs.
You do not hear me
breathing; my ache for touch
is more than tracery of ink.
The poem you did not read
is not an artifact or monument.
There is blood inside.

— Jan. 1982, rev. 2020

WHAT THE SACHEM'S SON TOLD ME

Westward, the packed
wagons, the loaded guns,
the sleep-soft watchfulness,
the hoarded-in dreams
of the White Man, west,
went from sea to great river,
from plain to mountain,
then to the final sea
at world's end.

They took it all:
the redwood groves,
pan-gold streams,
bottomless wells,
peat-soft soil,
the promised land of
no-questions equality.
For *them*.

Sometimes we managed
to curtail their dreams,
cutting them off
at the root of a scalp.
Our arrows vectored down,
our carnage a vortex
of vulture-spin and blood.
The earth drank them;
the sky
consumed their bones.
We kept the iron pots,
the buttons and pretty beads.
Their guns became ours.

In spite of that,
a thousand nations
became but one. They spoke
no other language but their own.

Our people are penned
in all the waste-places,
roach-motel reservations.
No arrow can stop
the six-wheeled megatrucks;
train tracks and highways vein
the former wilderness.

But as for you, poet:
Thank you for coming.
Know that our knives are drawn
and could take you out
in a minute, if so we chose.
But since you greeted us
with words you took
from our own language,
and since you are, like us,
of those who walk the dreams
and make them into magic,
we will walk in peace together.

Walk with me now,
away from the sage-smoke.
I will tell you
that our power is returning,
if we learn to wield it
without the white man's poison
forever weakening.

I have found something,
a survivor of totem days,
I have a manitou,
cousin of Wendigo, Hudson Bay's
wind-walker, elemental.
Cloud-lurker, he evens
the score. *Look up!*

The poet sees, in night sky, but lit
from underneath by earth-light,
an airplane departing
from the nearby airport.
"Watch!" the young Iroquois says.
A dark cloud envelops the DC-10 above.
One wing snaps off, and then
the other. It is all the more
horrible that the screams cannot be heard.

"Hunh!" is all the sachem's son utters.
"It gives me no pleasure.
I would rather the earth swallow them
of its own accord, and spare The People.
Our People, I mean."

"Do work on that," the poet urges.
"The outraged planet listens, I am sure."

A smile creases the cracked corners
of the wizard's otherwise humorless mouth.
"We will still keep their pots and pans,
the motor-bikes and the pretty beads.

"Come to the pow-wow now
and we'll get plenty drunk, poet!"

— *Oct. 1982, rev. 2020.*

NIAGARA AND BACK, 1966

With four days off
for holiday,
instead of turkey
and stuffing, my friend
and I decided to hitch-hike
Walt Whitman's open road.

To where? To nowhere
or anywhere! Let's see
how far we can go!

Five miles short
of Erie, a sailor,
on leave and adrift
on his own adventure,
picked us up.

Where to? he asked.
Where are you going?
we asked. *Niagara Falls,*
he said, *and all the way
into Canada.*

Wide-eyed, we said
in unison, *Then we
are going to the Falls.*
We all laughed.

He never talked
about his ship or where
it took him, whether
to Vietnam or some
safe coast patrol.

You didn't ask
why or what
soldiers might have seen
unless they wanted
to tell someone
and said so.

Arriving at the Falls
and its noisy grandeur
we thanked our driver
and parted ways. We made
our way along the banks
above the Falls,
defied the signs and scoured
the rocky river shore
for specimens. My friend
was a geology major
and knew what does
and doesn't belong.
I found a hollowed-out
rock almost too much
to carry about. He said
it was an Indian wheat-stone.
Into my bag it went.

Oblivious to borders
and needing no papers,
we crossed to Canada.
We sampled such food
as nearly indigent
students could afford,
then reveled in sunset
and the rainbow-lit
Falls, immense
and grander by far
from foreign vantage.

Taking a cue
from a "Rooms for Rent"
sign, we found a room,
a tiny attic garret
that cost as much
as what our two wallets
contained, sparing enough
for one tiny breakfast.

*You'll have to share
the one small bed,*
the landlady said.
It's the last room.
She winked at me.

In minutes we were in the dark
and under one tiny blanket.
My friend said,
If you touch me, I'll kill you.

So much for Walt Whitman.

Next morning we found
the cheapest diner
and spent our last coins
on bacon and eggs.

Hearing our talk,
the man next to us turned.

It was the sailor again.

Things didn't work out,
he said. *I'm heading back.
Are you guys staying or ...*

The unsaid was said
in that moment's pause.
Had *he* planned to desert
and changed his mind?
Were *we* across the border
to dodge the draft?[1]

We're going back, I said.

I'll take you back, then,
he offered. *I kind of need
the company, you know.*

At the border he showed
his military ID.
We two were asked
where we were born
and where we had been
on the Canadian side.

We went right through.
The sailor moved something
from under his seat
into the glove compartment.
Not to worry, he said.
It's not loaded.

It was a slow trip
southward. We stopped
at Buffalo. He bought
us a welcome lunch.
Then, long after dark
he left us along
a local road somewhere
north of Meadville.

---

[1] The U.S. drafted 382,010 men into military service in 1966, the highest total during the Vietnam War.

Fourteen miles to walk
in the November night!
The withered corn
leaned dead
into the frosty air.

Yellow lights beamed
from sheltered farms
across the stippled fields.

No cars came. Not one.
We heard no sound
save that of cows
stalking the brush
beside us,
they walked,
but kept their distance.
Not one of them
had ever gone astray.

At last, in despair,
we found a sheltered spot
behind a hay-pile
and curled up to rest.
My best friend
nestled behind me for warmth.

I gazed at the unsleeping stars.
You touch me, my friend said,
and I kill you.

Good night, I answered.

Fifty, a hundred
miles away, the sailor
pulled over on a dark road.
He reached for the gun.
Things didn't work out.

SUMMER OF 1967: CLEVELAND OHIO

Cityscape to townscape
  concrete to clapboard
    Cleveland to nameless tree-
      lined hydrant peppered
        dogwalk
streets seen from the blur of bus yet
  slowing, limning in slant
    of afternoon for me

twenty years old on my first journey West,
Walt Whitman's poetry open on my lap,
atop it the journal I am writing in

    this slice of nation:
the lonely boy on the porch
  this Ohio summer of '67
    looks up, sees me
      seeing *him,* writing
        him here on this page —

perched on this pile of Whitman,
  Connecticut Yankee, damnable
    Moby Dick (my transcon-
    tinental shelf of books)

And old Walt said: *look at him.*
  A long red light permitting, I looked.
  He smiled, not as if at any one
  of the tinted faces of dusty green
  Grey-monoxide-hound, but at *me* —
he regarded me as intently as I, him —

And Walt whispered:
There are wonderful secrets everywhere,
and one of them is that you and he are a poem.

Sidewalk — a boy and a girl
wave to the porch boy   he waves
    distractedly, still looking at me,
my eye locks on him as my pen
scribbles on, robotically.

My pen hand begins to tremble.
Oh, this moment, Walt!
Would that I had stopped and spoken to you,
blond Ohio, I think I might have loved you
    and you as well might have loved me!

I saw nothing else and hills
    turned to plains,
    to seas of swept green,
saw only eyes and a tousled-haired
    boy head blue-eyed with parted lips,
asking my name and *are we a poem?*

And would I not later find
that there are always eyes
that flash and promise everything,
and that I must do the same in return,
whatever the cost —

    at forty miles an hour and the states
    still whisking by, I am still thinking of him —

I marvel, but Walt has taught me well
already, that one can love so much
and be loved in an instant
of recognition.

Was he merely beautiful,
this never-forgotten fleeting one?
Or has he remembered the fire
of one glance that led him to books,
to a world beyond the lake-front porch?

And if the War did not come and take him,
did he not walk too with the good gray Poet
and make his way West to glory?

THINGS DONE IN CITIES

My Hudson-cliff view from Weehawken
does not efface the smear of it,
Manhattan clogged in its own soot,
the river gray-black with sinister flotsam.

The shade of sycamores and elms,
the brace of breeze and lambent sun,
the promise of golden reflections
if we wait for sunset — these things
cannot negate my friend Boria's lament:

"Peaceful from here, a birdflight
removed, a squint of street.
But still, the thought of the prostitutes,
the gaudy porno shops,
the thought of what might touch you
if you walked along Forty-Second Street.
How have we grown so base?"

I need but close my eyes
to remember slick Dimitrios
and his harem of underage
no-names, and how he sold
his brother's son to slavers
under the eyes of the officers.

Where?
On the steps of the Parthenon.

And when?
Just twenty-three times
a hundred years ago.

AFTER THE FUGUE IN B MINOR

You have emerged again from the fugue,
a phantom stepped out of counterpoint, at burst
of ominous pedal point, your ululating step
fringed with chromatics — I thought I had lost
your tenor in all that tumult, or in those rules
that ban our moving in parallel steps
or ever singing in unison,

but there you are, out-of-place,
a metaphor for lutes and panegyric hymns,
my untouched cipher whom I would decorate
with myrtle. Defy, if you dare, this
    separateness
that only a Lutheran cantor could
    want to impose.

Ah, you are gone again. I have lost you.
Our voices never cross; we move in our permitted
range, remotely similar, earthbound alike,
my bass aspiring to your fanciful curves,
you in the middle voice, keyboards above,
I in the plodding pedal, trapped below.

We stay alien as much to one another
as they who soar soprano must seem
to both of us. A fugue has a cruel beauty,
as strict as military order. Meet me here
at midnight, my elusive friend! Do not
fail to appear. The cantor will be asleep,
the minister well into his ale-house slumber.
Just us, and the organist,
in the dark of the moon. The bellows-boy
will be sworn to secrecy, and pump away!
And we, we shall be free to scamper and play,
chase one another and even embrace
in chord after chord, and leaping intervals,
all rules abandoned. *A Toccata! A Toccata!*

THE AGONY OF ORCHIDS

What can they mean to you,
this line of courtiers?

Why do they come and go
as though they had keys
of their own to your dwelling?

Do they not blush when they pass
one another in the stairwell?

So much simpler, so free
of collisions is our pact
of mutual avoidance!

There, floats another
in the nearby lagoon;
I hear tell of a self-hanging.

I leave to *them* the horror
of loving you

(they warm you
against the night-black chill
that is our greater love);

to *them*, the pain
of your gay dismissal,
to them, the anguish
   of your pearly laugh,

the agony of orchids
   you cultivate
   to bloom from suicides;

I leave to *them*
    the only fit reward
    for loving you —

a Carnival death,
knives drawn
    by unknown strangers
all with the same face,
identical daggers
thrust from gloved hands
in a whirl of black dominos.

I watch, I count,
I bide my time.

—1968/1979/1985, rev 2020

DEAD OF PROSE AT 29

*In memoriam, Stuart Milstein,
January 1977, aet. 29)*

1
A flash of light in his skull
and the bulb burned out,
the moth whose wingbeat
blinked in his eyes
has fled, the vacancy
of irises draw cold inside,
down veins into his arms.

He had turned his back on poems.
Fiction he would conquer,
and be a critic, too.
The typewriter hummed,
plots cooled, awaiting
a thrust, a denouement,
a theory to end all theories
that did not come.
The inkwell from which
the poems had come
was dry, a broil of verse
on scraps of notepads.

Five days the Muse came by
and knocked, pacing the hall
in fear and jealousy.
What was he doing?
Who did he think he was,
Dostoyevsky? Proust?
She hid on the stairs
when they broke down the door,
her cry a tiny lament
in their more shrill alarm.

Had he written himself to death?
This mortal coil so easily shed,
just after the tender leaves
of his tender books of poems
had broken the soil,
and withered, unnoticed.

Careless, somehow, of risk,
eschewing cures; a secret smile
at abandoned regimens,

he was a backslid vegetarian
inviting the tusks of herbivores;
and, epileptic,
he put aside his medicine.

He courted Death
in haze of Eden lost.
There had been a woman,
a European dark lady,
and all had not gone well.

Alone in Brooklyn at twenty-nine;
the knock at the door
three times,
   the dreaded Guest,
the flash in his brain,
no time to —

Alone in his book
his poems are glass:
inside, his eyes
stare back at us.
What is one to do
at such catastrophe?

His tiny book,
like all others,
is but an Icarus
in sun-fire.

Who reads? Who notices?
Who wants to meet us
because of the words we weave?

2
I was his publisher.
I carry his book about
like a little tombstone.

He was disconsolate
as we walked in Prospect Park
that no one had noticed
the few review copies
he had cajoled me to mail.
"It doesn't help," I told him.
"America hates poetry." —

"It doesn't help to be Jewish,"
he told me. Naïve, I answered,
"What does that mean? I envy
your being Jewish." — "How envy?" —
"You know who you are. You know
where your ancestors came from.
The rest of us doesn't even know
where our grandparents came from.
We are mostly barbarians."

He shook his head. I didn't understand
that even poetry could be consigned
to a ghetto, and in our time.

Poets must be made
of stronger stuff.
It is a life that chooses us,
and we must take it
with all its perils and costs.

The Muse is unforgiving,
and as for Prose,
    well, that will never do.

It is almost enough
to get you killed.

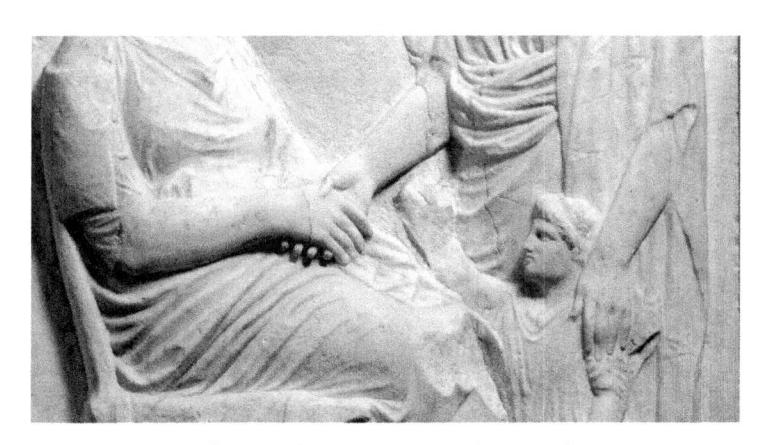

FATAL BIRDS
OF THE SOUL

FATAL BIRDS OF THE SOUL

An Experiment, after Rilke's Duino Elegies

1
ENVOI

Night. *Night.* Spring sleeps on ice below,
within the vaulted limestone corridors,
awaiting a birth. The Poet hesitates
to summon an equinoctial tempest,
for soon enough the seeds and homing birds
will make their own way back, unhelped.
He calls instead on Night to season him:
Night with its trembling hopes is his;

not Spring, whose promises are often false
(the open seed is never what the flowers
prophesied); not Summer, when green
and sun grow fat in gluttony of light;
not Fall, whose frost reaps only solitudes;
not even this Winter is really his.
(The glittering ice-eyed avenue cracks
at the edge of a thaw, more pastry-faced
than glacial). To Night alone,
the waxing-waning-equipoised base
of the spun year, he takes his oath.

Night. *Night!* Wherever his shadow falls,
    its kingdom precedes him;
wherever his pen dyes paper black,
    Night reaches up to etch itself.

2
YET ANGELS STALK

Lamp-lit, air in a tremolo of antique
instruments, he incubates the moment,
the blast of elegance that renders vowels
oversize, enlarging thought and form.

Who, if he cried, would hear among
the order of Angels? Which one among their
multitudes would answer him? (One,
he would guess, whose amplitude
he had already loved in resemblances!)

Love at first sight — what is it
but the eye-dart of the un-met Angel?

And what if one of these beings
should suddenly arrive and press
its form and frame against his heart?
His breath would stop. He'd fade into
the strength of its starker essence,
blinded and numbed by possibilities.
All those he ever thought he knew
enough to love them, are swept away,
in the light-blast of a single sentience.

There is no God, yet Angels stride
the emptiness of stars. He apprehends
that Beauty, angel-possessed
     abstractedness,
is but a clue to that deep nullity;
for Beauty is nothing but tentative Terror
he's still just able to bear. Why he adores
it so is that its lassitude deigns not
to destroy him. Even one Angel
     is terrible.

He looks up, and looks at it,
and for a while, returns to writing.
There is a poem, after all, to finish,
the summoned inner voice must have
its full until the rounded line is reached.

His reticence, as the Angel watches
patiently, lets it suffice that such Beauty
is seen from the corner of one eye;

it is well that he does not speak to It,
letting the pen invoke his terror,
spare him the muffled croak of sobbing.

(O Love that has gone before,
to and beyond the tomb,
this is no harbinger of reunion!
We who have lived with raven
and crow and the lurking vulture
take no comfort from wingbeats.)

Night. *Night*. Let the Angel come sideways,
halo'd at the edge of vision, winged
but still as the sculpted head of Hermes
that flickers on his candled book-case.

Let the Angel come gradually. Let him wait
until the pen is closed, the manuscript
turned over so the dead may read it
as their faces press upward; let it wait
until he stands, and bows & makes inquiry
on what business an Angel should be about.

3
HIS, THE DEEP NIGHT

Night. *Night.* Wary of those who come
with just a midnight's yearning, he waits
for sign or sigil, a blazon'd sword or staff.
Nothing. White dust in air would be
as vague, white chalk on board left ghost
by hurried erasure, as legible. What use,
this Angel, if the being is what he appears?
Men have given him little, books much.
What could an incorporeal creature tell him?
How readily these sentient ones,
these brutish Gabriels with perfect teeth,
perceive our need, and our world-malaise.
Here one moment, and gone the next,
Angels alienate; they make us doubt
the truth of the sight-interpreted world.

Words up *his* sleeves, the poet knows
how artfully we weave our sights into
        transcendent cloaks.
There lingers, perhaps, and taking root
for more than its outward worth
the Ordinary made Sublime:
some tree on a hill, to be seen
each day with new utility and hope;
the counterfeit loves that arrived
during yesterday's walk, now pressed
between denials and dried;

    add, too, the old housebroken loyalty
of habits that liked him and stayed
and never gave notice, and, finally,
that half-a-world that he envelops at dusk,
already his kingdom with no admittance
required by benediction or grace, *his*,
the Night, *his* the deep Night,
when pin-prick wind

feeds on his face from cosmic spaces.
He looks at it; the Angel regards him.
There is no gesture of going, or staying.
He has not offered it a chair, nor poured
a second cup of tea (as if a phantom
needed rest or stimulant!). It has not smiled
or offered a word of comfort. Male
or female, being of dark or light,
mute if messenger, closed hands
and clenched jaw not of caresses
made or expected, for whom
would this dis-enchanter
stay? longed for by all, painfully draped
from trees for lonely hearts to admire —
if it is not about love, what is it?

Somewhere in a ruined abbey
is a black, unyielding bell,
its clapper of life long gone, so that
nothing save the hammer-blow
of final Apocalypse can ring it.

He thinks, *Can this be lighter for lovers?*
Does the Angel come with a clarion,
the high trilling of silver bells?
Go off then, he thinks. *Your business
is with some fool in love, not me.*

Lovers! They only deceive themselves!
When will they learn? Throw out your
loneliness: it is but air from the absence
    of arms to encircle you.
Exhale the idea. Gift it to birds —
at least they will use the lift of it for flight.

4
WHAT IS A POET FOR?

Springs needed him. Stars arching up
from winter sleep awaited the names
with which he'd anchor them. What
is a poet for? Waves from the past
anticipated the nights he'd call them back.
Sometimes, on city street, he'd hear
a violin surrender itself to bow and arm
behind an open window-way. What
is a poet for? to make of anything
and everything a Heaven, all with words;
to beat down Hell, if that is what
the story indicates. This was entrusted him,
and a few others before and after.
But he seldom equaled it. Was he
not always led off by expectations,
made the fool by mere coincidence,
as though all this were signaling
there was someone he was supposed
to love? (He stalked immensities
on his pages, but lovers stalked *him,*
their shaggy sentiments going in and out,
and sometimes even staying
until the sparrows awoke him).

If even *one* were love, why did
those pages piled high not earn
and keep some fair companion? Why now
this incorporeal Angel accusing him?

5
THE ARROW ENDURES

One arm extended, the Angel advances,
and places on the poet's paper'd table,
a single, silver arrow, fletched in black.
No blood has stained its point or shaft.

He gazes in terror and fascination:
no sword is as mighty as his wielded pen,
but as for Love's arrow —

When longing seized him, late at night
in the final ache before sleeping, he sang
of great lovers: the fame of all they felt
is never immortal enough that he could not
add to its luster among the fixed stars.
He almost envied some of them (Antony
and his Egyptian queen, dead Romeo
and expiring Juliet, the unforgettable and
unpursued Beatrice, leading Dante on),
especially the forsaken ones enduring
beyond the need for requited love. Each verb
of his verse aspired to unattainable praise
for them. He did not mourn the Hero,
but Lovers whom we have utterly lost.
Exhausted Nature takes them back
without transforming them again,
dead in a sunken city,
dead in a ruined tomb,
dead despite the ascent to Purgatory's
heights. Dead at the beginning
of love instead of at the end
of a long life of mutual devotion.

He held their valiant possibilities
and revered them; wished that his own
old sufferings could yield such fruit.

To one afar, who shunned him,
to another, already entombed,
had he not written in his lines,
In Love's name I abjure you.
Let me instead be like
those valiant doomed lovers.
Is it not time I freed myself
from you, and, quivering,
>   *endured?*

But there, the Arrow before him.
If in his name it had flown,
it had reached no one;
if aimed for him, it lay there
unshot, unclaimed and pure.
Where was the bow, the quiver,
the bold arm tensed, the eye
with perfect aim, the string
whose one vibration would fell him?

The Arrow endured the string,
fell somewhere where the Angel
acquired it and came as messenger.
In this, its conciliated leap,
it was much more than itself.

An arrow, motionless, is sad.
It knows that staying
is nothingness.

6
THE FATE OF LOVERS

What is the fate of Lovers, then?
Denied themselves, do they requite
the emptiness that aches for *them?*
We know the ordinary dead
tap roots into our heritage, lend us
their wrinkles year by year.
Sometimes they wear us like shoes.

But lost to us totally,
do Lovers scour asteroids of dust,
searching the trace of anterior flight
of a belov'd? How else but by
their space-stretched amplitude
could they be heard?
                      They *are* heard.
Poets are the drum-skin
   of dead lovers' timpani.

7
THE DOOM OF SAINTS

He believed in love, but only that
of mortal souls for one another,
or of one mind for the Infinite.

And yet there were voices,
voices, heard in his heart
as only saints have heard.
Like them, he was lifted aloft,
but unlike them he looked
the Lifter unafraid, and eye-to-eye.

(Poor Saints, *they* did not want to see,
went right on kneeling, in cumulus,
in stratosphere, blinded by vows,
o never this, o never that,
no idle pleasure for thee or me,
right up to the final esplanade of stars.

Of self-effacing faith, beware!
Saints never knew those glints are teeth,
or how the lips of God upcurl
as He devours them like grapes.)

A Saint is a soul's abortion.

8
NIGHT OF THE YOUTHFUL DEAD

No, the voices he hearkens to
are yet another suspiration of Night:
the words that come to him as though
dictated in someone's voice, the words
that proceed from nothing.

Poets who died young
may be the most persistent
phantoms, moth-wings against
the vision of the still-living.

He knows that the Night
   is also peopled with Angels,
whatever they are, that lines
of youthfully dead pour into it
and may be one and the same.
(One time beneath the open dome
    of a Roman church,
its incensed shadow spilled into Night,
even though it was noon outside
and he felt the darker cherubim steal in
and quietly address his solitude.)

What did they want of him?
Why should he hold them back
with his compassionate hopes,
from their procession to purer heights?

And why, if he addressed them,
should they consent to answer him?
They are about their business,
the solemn business of being dead.
What could they possibly want
that anyone could offer them?

9
To Loneliness

He thinks, but does not say:
*Angel, leave me. You have
no words to lend me, no hand
with willing grasp to lead me
to table, bed, or precipice.
I am defined by solitude!*

How common is loneliness,
sadness in singleness, unique
yet everywhere alike!
No census counts it,
yet its needs outweigh
all measure and taxation.

Everything with a name
is lonely. Call not a thing
a member of its class only,
assembly-line identical:
no, each and every thing
lives in a solitude entire,
a dim and fading aureole
of assured existence. The stars
with all that space between
are lonelier than we;
and surely the last
great condor is lonely
on his volcano peak.

The crying child fears
that no one will come,
molds in his heart
the carbuncle of singularity.
The well-loved wife,
each moment her back is turned
from her constant husband,
holds within her a loneliness

like a still-born egg;
the revered grandfather
surrounded by progeny,
looks off afar and sees it all
as no assuage for the void
inside his ever-stirring soul.
He wanted more; he settled
for this, and these, and
what was it all for?

The more the crowd, the more
the weight of solipsist woe
that none are real, that nothing *is*
except one's inner emptiness,
the Ego's echo chamber.

He does not fear this. His drear
self-haunted palace is all he knows.
All art is loneliness.
Why sex is at the center
of everything is that
it is the loneliest act:
completion's quest,
conquest's charade,
the pride of possession's
protectorate, the final ache
of disillusion. No poem
can be as lonely or sad
as a kiss.

VIXI ALIIS DVM VITA FVIT,
POST FVNERA TANDEM
NON PERII, AT GELIDO
IN MARMORE VIVO MIHI;
HELMANVS GVLIELMVS ERAM
ME FLANDRIA LVGET;
HADRIA SVSPIRAT;
PAVPERIESQ VOCAT-

OBIIT XVI KAL:OCTOB:
CIƆ IƆ XCIII.

10
THE INSCRIPTION

The everyday Angels do not speak.
Far from it — God's voice,
even at second-hand,
could not be endured.
Enough it is to hear the ever-
repeated speech that silence brews,
to watch their flying-saucer halos
flutter about like circus hoops
for the high trees' nervous sparrows.

Words from the mouths of those
youthfully dead still hover there
in consecrated space, raising
his hair and bristling at edge
of audibility. In Rome
and Naples did not these hesitant
shades call out to him each time
he entered a quiet church?

Or else an inscription imposed
sublimer thoughts on him, as one
upon a tablet in Santa Maria Formosa:

While I had life I lived
for others' sake; now dead,
I have not perished, but
live for myself in marble cold.
Hermanus Gulielmus I was.
Now Flanders mourns me,
now Hadria sighs,
and Poverty calls for me.
Died 16th October in 1593.

11
THE INVITATION

Is he to join them? Is that the intent
of his silent messenger, the arrow
he might into his own heart stab,
the imploring look in the Angel's eyes?

It's true, it would be strange
to leave the earth behind,
to inhabit the spaces between, and times
beyond the ken of clocks, to use
no more the customs just barely assumed.

To be a poet and yet refrain
from defining a rose, or other signs
that meant so much with a human future
stretched out as a road to travel on;
to be eased away from callings
too cleverly laced with old knots,
to put aside one's proper name
like a broken or outgrown toy,
no longer to wish or want, lacking
the means to keep a feather aloft!

What if not one page of his writing
survived to be read aloud
from one reader to one listener —
would it matter so much?

Strange, being intangible, how objects
once clear to one lose meaning or name.
What is a *house*, in fact, once one
can walk upon, within or under it
with no regard for gravity and mass?

It must be hard for the dead,
so full of lingering, to lift
their little spark of eternity

and finding it, pass on!
The too-fine lines the living draw
must hamper them — it's said
some Angels fail to know they're dead,
but move as easily with us
as with their own.

Were the Egyptians right, then,
that the worthy dead, with liberated *ka,*
could walk freely among the living?
And could one dwell among those dead
one always wanted to greet and thank?

What if, instead, and much to dread,
this was but Angels' adolescence?
And what if what they passed to next
was the utter hell of oblivion, the blot
of nonexistence, less essence left
than that of the humblest pebble?

What if the Wind,
born of black ebon'd space,
whirls time through either realm,
parching the voices of angels and men.

What if at last,
in need of us no more,
the early-departed
are gently weaned from the earth,
just as the child outgrows the breast?
Even the dead young poet, gone
after a while into nothingness!

O guest, I abjure your arrow!
Angel, I would not have
your fleeting, evanescent,
firefly, will-o'-the-wisp beauty.
Tempting it is to fly with you,
tempting it is, but, No!

12
NOT OF THIS EARTH

For who would wish, finally,
to be not of this earth?
Oh, some, in secret, name that wish
yet dare not seek it —
to be unearthed, unpeopled,
free of relatedness.

Could he exist without the world,
when he dredged even his tears
lest even one sad truth elude him?
Could one abandon geodes,
maples and butterflies, the orchid
and its blunt, admiring bromeliad?
The mountain, and its shadow;
the lake, and the sky within?
Disowning earth, he would shed
the very sorrow that charged him.

Why should we mourn the dead?
Oh, it is thousand times more
the dead should mourn the world
that can no longer hold them!

Was it in vain that primal notes,
in mourning for Linos, first pierced
the rhythmless air, that song
Ai Linos! that prompts the question
"Just who was Linos, anyway?"
Unwanted infant of a priestess
seduced by Apollo, he was exposed
on a hillside for devouring dogs.
For the dogs' repast, the god
set plague upon Argos,
whose mothers and fathers sang
Ai Linos! until the wrath had passed.

Where now, the abandoned children,
where, the shunned dead
    in their mass graves?
Does any lament or requiem rise,
or do they fall, dead-weight
upon the hearts of mourners?

Was it in vain that the horrified space
a nearly-deified boy
quite vanished from, should feel,
in the repeated lament,
Ai Linos, some throb of melody
that charms us and comforts and helps?

What if it comforts no one?
What if each Angel is itself alone?
What if they have not even
    each other's company?

What if the Angel's news
about the beloved is:
he was not there, he is not here.

What else is Death
but a thief in the night?

13
FATAL BIRDS OF THE SOUL

Still, single, silent Angel,
the poet finds you terrible.
Though he invokes you
above and beyond his gods
and monsters, daemons and Muses,
he knows what you are, you
all-but-fatal birds of the soul,
taunting and ineluctable.

These are not the days of Tobias
when one of the glowing host
came to his door in Nineveh,
barely disguised for traveling,
his wings and aureole concealed
in rough robes, not awesome —
a youth to the youth
as he glanced out at him.

Let some Archangel today,
slipping behind a star
assume humanity
and see what happens!

Doubts, dreams, flashbacks
to bad hallucinations, more rival myths
than fingers could count, self-doubt,
the viewing of stars through prisms,
the all-too-proven knowledge of atoms,
of the full spectrum's sweep
from infra-red to gamma rays.

Where does even a well-decked Angel
fall in this scheme of things?
From where does he say he comes?
What stellar coordinates?

And does he utter his warning
in Greek or Aramaic? Does one need
an interpreter for more than hand-signs?
Oh, if he but loved life, and knowing,
less — if he had not read *Faust* entire—

then might his winged heart burst
to fly to the Angel!

14
SPAWN OF THE ELDER GODS

What if the form of the Angel
is only a perpetrated fraud,
like Zeus to Ganymede or Semele,
assuming whatever guise
the viewer most wishes to see?

He leans toward the Angel
and says the unspeakable:

You who take the shape
of an Angel, show yourself!
Shape-shifting spawn of the Elder Gods,
what are you, really? Older than man,
unguessable experiments of form and mass,
early successes pampered by gods,
high crags and ranges tipped red
by the dawn of the world,
summits of all beginning
draining the sun
into your nascent hearts?

What would I see,
if I saw you plain and true?
Mute, sleeping rocks in space?
Or vesicles of gray, tentacled gods?
Hinges of light at rainbow doors,
stairways and halls, thrones
vacant or filled with amber mists,
spaces for beings invisible and sere
yet not the entities themselves?

If you are messengers of glory
yet represent only the universe,
blaze on and tell me. I can bear the truth.
Is there joy in tapestries of stars, a shield
reflecting happiness alone
in some distant Eldorado,
braziers of rapture storming up,
and there, apart from all,
at the core of being and its eidolons,
the mirrors that draw your faces up
and bring them back to me
as actual beauty, not counterfeit.

It is above all essential
that the Beautiful be true.

15
THE LOVE OF THE BEAUTIFUL

He did not blame the Angel
if it wore the mask of Hermes.
If an ugly Angel came,
   who would believe it?

For did he not persuade himself
that each he loved was beautiful?
Even if others told him otherwise!
And how does one attain the love
of the beautiful without an equal
share when he faced his mirror?
A plain creature with mouse-brown hair,
how much could he claim and hold?

Yet he, when he felt, could evaporate,
could don imaginary armor, and dare.
He breathed his essence out and away,
each ember a fainter glow and fire.
He could die of it, this longing.

Though someone who came and stayed
once told him, "You're in my blood,
this room and even the Spring
is full of you," he did not believe it.

What use? For who could hold
anyone? Those desperate embraces
meant to encircle him become engulfed
by his own imagination.

And who could hold another back
if he is endowed with beauty,
if ideal lines incessantly slant
across his brow — like dew
on the morning grass, or heat
from a smoking dish? Gone
like a smile or an upturned glance
that never returns to its maker,
gone in the diminishing waves of the heart,
gone in those fading sighs that left him.

16
SOME HINT OF US

Does emptiness, in making way
for our advance, taste of us, then?
Do Angels only claim their own
of us, restoring what had streamed
from them, or does an oversight
catch up a little of ourselves as well?
Have we in their outgoing forms
some hint of us, such as the look
that vaguely haunts the visages
of pregnant wives, marked not
by them in their whirl
to return to themselves?
(Why should they perceive it)?

Does sight, the undelivered Arrow,
turn only back upon itself?
The Poet, assured of his own
existence, what else can he know?

17
LIKE ZEPHYR'D AIR

Lovers, perhaps, if Angels understood,
might utter marvels at midnight's peal.
But all conspires to hide us.

You see, the trees exist, so too
the houses we live in go on
from day to day. We only pass
the whole world by like zephyr'd air.

And all as one they hem us in,
somewhat as shame perhaps,
and partly as inexpressible hope.

Why place is at the heart
of fiction, is that all tales
are rooted to the ground like trees.

The ruined Abbey, the smothering
tomb, the riverbank from which
the fatal asp is gathered up —
all are the fatalities of landscape.

The tellers of tales must tell
the tales they tell, and no others.

An oak can no more pine cones
make than a pine, an acorn.

Why Love is at the heart
of poetry, is that its ground
is everywhere, and nowhere.

18
THE TOUCHING PERSISTS

Lovers, I question you,
so satisfied in one another:
reveal us all.

You hold yourselves! What proof?
My hands sometimes become aware
of one another — sometimes my
weary face drops down between
the two of them. That too
is a sensation I feel. From that,
I ask, can I presume I exist?

You, though, who in the other
grow rapturous, till overwhelmed
you cry, "No more"; who under
each other's hands grow rich
like wines of vintage years;
sinking, sometimes, but only because
the other has surfaced again:
it's you I ask to define us. No need
to ask why you so blissfully touch:
because the touching persists,
because the spot you cover
so tenderly
will never move; because
you seem to see in it a grasp
upon enduring — in an embrace
almost a token of eternity.

Yet is it so? Once you survive
first contact's fear, the watchful longing
at half-drawn shades, and that first walk,
just one, when first you link an arm
into each other's solitude: now, Lovers,
are you the same? Now when you lift
yourselves to drink each others' lips —
kiss unto kiss — how strangely now
the drinker eludes the drink!

The far-off look of the accustomed
lover, the averted eye
(there, each sees it in the other!),
sighs without object — Oh, do not place
the Infinite into a wine-glass!

19
THE RENEWING KISS

Are these high moments reserved to youth,
dimming as beauty dims, wrinkling
and gray? For when our elder selves
aspire to that renewing kiss, we seek it
in youths, not in our own. Youths,
yes, who close their eyes to us or pass
their heat into to our bones oblivious.
The old are but the house-cats of Death.

Beauty, the fragile deity we house,
comes in like birds, sings, mates;
some never leave, while others fly
and drop their broken shells behind.
All we can do is wear them well,
the shards and gifts they give us,
adoring Beauty wherever it comes to rest,
and pray the grace and dignity
to know *it* flies,
while we remain below.

Marble grave stele with a family group, c. 360 BCE.
Metropolitan Museum, New York.

20
LOVE AND FAREWELL

On Attic funerary stones,
did not the gestures amaze
you with their evasiveness? were ever
Love and Farewell so lightly laid
upon shoulders? they seemed to be made
of other stuff than we are,
seem too in their suggestiveness
of no touch at all, to contradict
the weight and bulk of stone.

The touch, perhaps, was in the rock
the sculptor chipped away.

Remember the hands
that rested weightlessly,
though power spilled from the torsos!

The truth of what they withheld was this:
that even so cautiously we mortals
must venture to touch, and no more.

21
CODA:
THE UNDELIVERED MESSAGE

Night. *Night.*
One Angel. One Arrow.
One Poet. The Angel, mute.
If there was a message,
    it was not delivered.
The Arrow never reached
its target. Perhaps, like
Zeno's arrow,
perpetuum mobile,
it is infinitely delayed.
Perhaps no thrum of bow
has ever resounded,
no vector drawn
from eye of Lover
    to the Beloved.

The Arrow is the enigma
of longing unfulfilled.
The Poet remains,
    transfixed between
unspeaking messenger,
and an act whose immanence
pounds at the door of non-Being.

If even one Angel is terrible,
how much more so is
an Angel inexplicable,
the frozen Arrow between
the actor and acted-upon.

(Dante, to love
    and to do nothing about it,
is Purgatory enough!)

What hangs in the scales
    in perfect balance
is the gap between two
    extended hands
that never come to touch.

BUSTER, OR THE UNCLAIMED URN

AN UN-ILLUSTRATED BOOK
by ABADON BARR-HALL

A posthumous collaboration
with
BARBARA A. HOLLAND

1.
A well-pleased gray cat gave birth
to a litter of fourteen little kittens
whose eyes were as yet unopened,
and who spent most of their days
crawling all over one another
while batting those who climbed over them
with their tiny paws, and sucking
the fresh milk from their mother's side.
One was a very special cat, not like
a cat that anyone had seen before.
Which one of the fourteen was he? We'll see!

2.
Then one day the lady who owned
their mother decided she only wanted *three*,
and would give *six* away to people
who would love them. And she would drown
the other five, for who would be
expected to take home so many kittens?
Too many, no matter how pretty
they all might be! Was he to be one
of the Chosen, or the Drowned?

3.
So the lady chose which kittens
she wanted. Most you could not tell
what gender they were as yet. Two were girls,
for sure, and one was a boy, and he was a noble
little thing. As pretty as anything could be.
Wasn't he the lucky one?

The doorbell rang. The visitors came.
They picked and chose and argued.
Even his mother was taken away.
The rest were scooped up. The toilet flushed.
Now he was the only one left! Just one!

4.
A voice in a tall shadow named him "Buster."
Buster was gray, silvery-gray
on the legs and back, gray on the back
of his head and his ears, but his face
was white, and he was white beneath
the chin and his chest and stomach,
and he wore white socks. What kind
of cat was Buster anyway, all this-and-that?

5.
Buster paid court to the woman,
big hands and shadow, loud voice and all.
He was hungry a lot.
Buster would wake the lady up
in the morning by licking her face
with his tongue. He patted her cheek
just ever so gently with his paws.
Buster had to pretend to like her,
or he would never get fed.

6.
Then came the day when the lady noticed
that he was fat for a kitten. Some sort of lump
stuck out at each side of his head,
and his forelegs met at two bent shoulders.
"That's not what a cat
is supposed to look like!" she muttered.
Whatever could be wrong with Buster?

7.
So then one day, when she was playing with him,
her fingers slipped along his sides
and she discovered that he had WINGS,
two little furry wings which fit him perfectly.
They were gray on the backs
and as he flapped them open,
they showed clean white beneath them.
Whoever heard of a cat with WINGS?

8.
Buster's head drooped on his chest.
She had discovered his secret.
Now she would drown him too,
for she hated everything that was not nice,
anything irregular or lumpy or out-of-shape.
He knew from what she said that *he* —
he was the only one of his brothers
and sisters and kittens of uncertain
gender, the only one for sure with WINGS!

He had another secret, too. He had WINGS,
and he knew how to use them!

9.
Would she hate him now? Would he be drowned?
But no, the lady seemed delighted. She crowed.
He lifted his head and looked straight at her.
"Go ahead," she said. "Show me."

Flapping his wings slowly, he showed her,
how up and out they opened, and flapped.
WINGS were to show you are happy.

10.
Each morning, he would get up,
stand on two legs as tall as he could,
and stretch his wings out, out and up.
He would set them shaking.
"Go ahead!" she encouraged him.
She laughed and he walked and fluttered.

Then down he went, like a common house-cat,
and all he could do was utter a faint *meow*.
The reward was a pat on his neck
and a trip to the bowl in the kitchen.
"My little eagle!" she crooned. "My little eagle."

11.
One day the windows were all-the-way open.
He walked to the far wall, then turned
and raced toward them and spread his wings
and FLAP, FLAP, FLAPPED
and he found himself flying out the window
just like the birds who fell by accident
and always seemed to come back up.

Now he knew their secret, too: up and out,
then down and up again! Imagine,
a cat with wings! No one was ever
going to drown him! And he had a world to see,
and his whiskers thrilled and trembled.

<232>

12.
Cats are no more curious
than any other animal,
    but a cat's WHISKERS
are like a personal radar.
Buster's seemed to feel about in the air.
They looked eager to understand.
Buster let the soft plume
of his tail stand straight up tall.
Now he could fly straight. This little thing
would make a difference.
Wings out, tail up, here comes BUSTER!

13.
He came and went from the house
without the lady knowing it —
she liked the window open,
and so did he. Back in the house
he was hearth-kitten, ears up and ready
for the sound of cat-food, for whatever sounds
were there to be heard, nose twitching for
fresh smells of clean litter and Lysol.

He did his duty when the lady entered.
"How is Buster? How is the little eagle."
Flap-flap-flutter-meow, he would answer.
He rolled on the floor, this way, that way,
wings tucked neatly under, resting up.

14.
Daytimes, when the lady went to work,
he had all the outdoors to investigate.
One night, on the window-sill, he heard
things he had never heard before,
a far-away fluttering, calling, the night,
the opal eye of the big moon,
so he slipped out the window
      and flew away.

She watched him do it. She ran to stop him.
She cried hopelessly,
for she thought he was gone for good.
No one was safe at night in the city!
Would Buster come back? Would you?

15.
But he was only just down in the garden,
three floors below where the ground-floor tenant
had roses (ouch!) to land on, soft ferns
and a catnip patch much visited by felines
of every conceivable shape and color.
There, he learned new ways to catch food.

16.
There were big ailanthus trees
all around the garden. They smelled terrible,
but up in their spiky leaves a person who flew
could get lost, or stay hidden
where no one would ever find them.
Among the flickering leaves at night,
only the eyes of the ones up there were visible.
Can you see BUSTER in the high trees?

17.
And there, one night, on a high branch,
he met a new friend, The Owl
(What owl? *Who?* Don't ask an owl his name
because he'll never tell you. *Who* will suffice.)
He doesn't talk much, anyway,
looks wiser and smarter than he actually is.
Turning his eyes this way, that way,
all he is thinking about is, probably: mice.

And that was just fine with Buster.
Buster loved mice.

18.
Buster knew one way only
to catch a mouse: a slow process
with no promise of getting anything,
just crouching in front of a hole
in the lady's baseboard, and waiting.
It had been hardly worth the trouble.

Out here, the mice were everywhere.
They ran about like crazy people,
looking for their own food. Careless,
they never saw Buster crouching
and certainly never saw The Owl
as he swooped down on them.

19.
Buster and the Owl, the Meow and the Who,
came up with a method to hunt together.
They'd hide among the leaves,
    The Owl, watching
    Buster, with his big ears and radar whiskers,
        listening. They made
a game of it, to see who could slide out
of the twig-end of the low branch first
and land on the back of the prey.

One mouse for you, Mr. Owl. One vole for you,
    Mr. Cat! The chipmunk is on to us.
A rat? A rat we can divide between us!

20.
Exploring the neighborhood by daytime
Buster would see bats like empty bags hanging
from the doors of old garages.
There goes one he frightened with his paw-prod:
no bigger than a mouse
but with a wingspread many times wider
than its little body.

Ah, Buster, marveled. If a cat can fly,
why not a mouse, a flying mouse?
These, Buster would not eat:
      he respected them.

21.
Birds! Oh to catch a bird!
Birds, after all, despite their prettiness,
devoured one another. One giant hawk
swooped down and made off with anything
its talons could carry: rabbits and birds,
chipmunks, and even a toy poodle
(to that, Buster said *Good riddance!*).
Buster wasn't good at catching birds.
He had been brought up for stalking.

22.
On a long flight
that nearly exhausted him
he came to a pond, and to a bird,
a lordly bird on stilts. The Heron
nodded a little and then resumed
his absolute stillness.

Buster saw fish, red, gold and brown
move aimlessly around the heron's legs.
How do you catch fish?
	he asked the Heron.

Hours and hours he stood and waited,
	the Heron explained
until the fish ignored him.
Then he'd jab down with his long beak
and come up with a neatly-skewered fish.

Buster did not have a beak,
and the water, which he tried,
was cold and chilling. Pads of his paws
could tread on water, he could dart
and flutter and try to catch fish,
but no, Buster was not getting wet,
the way the lady sometimes had tried,
with a bath, to make him clean and fluffy.

No way, Baby, no way
is any self-respecting cat
going to lurk in the water
on four short legs!

23.
He spent the summer
in the trees with all the varied birds
(they finally came to be unafraid
once he announced he couldn't catch them
and didn't like the taste of feathers, anyway.)
Well-fed on mice, he was growing.
He started to feel that time was passing.
He was bigger, stronger, longer-legged
and sleek, but something was wrong:
Buster's wings did not grow with him.
They were just the same size
as when he first kitten-flew
and made his great escape.

If this kept up, he would not lift himself
to the treetops anymore.

24.
On one final flight to see how far, how high,
how much of the city he could explore,
Buster flapped up to where a high wind
grabbed him and took him up *there*
to the dizzy-up where the hawks went.

His mouth wide, his whiskers extended,
tail up to guide him, he soared the skyline.
Towers he saw from above, rooftops and ladders,
windows and fire escapes, twisted iron ropes
of river-spanning bridges. Sharp edges, high
spires jabbed at him. If he fell here,
the city below would skin him alive.

25.
Buster was dizzy. He had gone too high.
No one should see their high places upside-down.
His wings were tired. He dropped
onto a window-ledge some thirty floors
above the street. He looked below
and almost belched a fur-ball. He looked
to both sides: nothing, just other windows
and no way to get to them.
What would become of Buster, thirty floors up?

26.
This was no place for a cat at all.
Balanced on three feet like any other cat,
he tapped with one forepaw
    against the window pane.
Buster was frightened now.
He remembered how The Owl had warned him:
Fur is no replacement for feathers.

He had lost his nerve for leaping.
Too high, too far,
    to the unforgiving pavement.
And no time to wonder if The Owl was wrong.

27.
Not every wind is friendly. New ones swirled
around the building, and lashed him.
The pigeons he shared the ledge with
kept nudging him, afraid
he would bother their little nestlings.
Move over, they said, or *fly back
    to where you came from.*
So Buster's ledge-hold became
a paw-and-claw tango.
If Buster fell off, could he fly up again?

28.
Inside the window a woman typed,
click-clickedly-clack, all the while Buster
was going *tap-tappedy-tap* at the window-pane.
He tried his loudest meow. The woman
looked up. She stared at Buster
in wide-eyed astonishment.

He kept one paw up
against the glass, as if to wave.
She didn't seem to see his wings
outstretched in desperation.
Instinct took over. She raised the window.
Into her two arms he leaped.
"Oh kitty!" she murmured.
"How did you get here, thirty floors up?"
Buster gave her his most
    consoling and grateful purr.

Soon the woman and her boyfriend
went off to the elevator (a car that went up
and down without a step or wing-beat!),
Buster held tight in their hands.
The door opened and closed.
Another man got on.
Cat-whiskers knew they were descending.
What would Buster's new friends do with him?

29.
Buster shook out his wings, just in case.
The stranger's voice bellowed, "What's that?
What are you doing with that huge bird
on this elevator?" "It's a CAT," the secretary
told the loud man, lifting up Buster
to the man's steel-gray eyes and moustache.
"He landed in fright on the window ledge.
We're bringing him down the street," explained
the young man. And Buster purred.

30.
Man, woman and cat emerged
into a noonday crowd below.
She petted Buster. The man's hands
began to tighten around Buster's
middle. His wings felt squashed.

"A winged cat! A feline Pegasus!
We're going to make a fortune on him,"
the man said. "We need a big cage.
I have a friend at the zoo. We'll be famous!"

And then in a burst of light and wind
they were outdoors. Buster went limp.
The woman yelled "Taxi! Taxi!"
With teeth and claws and wing-beat
Buster attacked the man and broke free.

He heard them screaming far below.
He was going home. He was fed up with flying.
People were no good, but at least
he had a place to be a hearth-cat.
His little wings had served him well enough.

31.
The lady's window was open.
When she saw Buster, she was so glad
she even sang a song. Never had he seen
so much milk, so big a bowl of food
(no mice, but what could one expect?)

She held him and held him,
and then she noticed. "Your wings!
They seem to be growing shorter
as your body grows bigger and bigger.
I wonder what a vet would say?"

32.
To say he did not like the "cat carrier"
was putting it mildly. And what did Buster
know about this creature called "The Vet"?
"These are vestigial wings," the Vet explained
as his gloved hand held Buster expertly.
"This is a full-grown cat you have here,
fully matured. He's a full-fledged tomcat now."

The woman paused to take that in.
She wrinkled her nose.
"How can I deal with that?"

"We can remove the vestigial wings,
so he's less likely to run into danger.
God only knows what he did while he was out there."

"Remove them? You mean a surgery?"

"Yes. Since he means so much to you."

"Of course," she gulped. Numbers they talked,
and then they went aside and whispered.

All Buster heard was, "The other thing
we can take care of while he's out."

33.
Babyhood, childhood, adolescence, all
were now in Buster's past. He was a new thing,
something they called a tom-cat. Did this mean
no more hunting for mice and voles and rats?
no more night-watch in tree-top with Mr. Owl?

Buster waited in a small cage.
Another cat, an orange tabby, howled
and meowed in the next cage.
They talked. The orange fellow — Max
was what his owner called him —
was here for an operation, too.
"Just you wait," Max said ominously.
I know what they do here. It's my turn now.
They're going to cut me down below.
I will no more go out a-prowling. No lady
cats in my future. And I will grow
immensely fat, and be pampered."

34.
"I'm here for something else," said Buster.
He flapped his wings to show what he meant.
"Harrumph!" said Max. "That's fine enough
to have a bird-part removed. Who needs it?
But no one leaves here without being *snipped*.
It's a conspiracy, and the Vet is a monster."

Buster had always wondered
what the she-cats and he-cats did in the alley
that made so much noise. His life as a cat
was about to be terminated.
All the lady wanted was the *idea* of a cat.

Buster decided he would rather be dead.

35.
Buster was pierced with a needle, and then another.
His vision spiraled down to darkness.
His wings were carved off, the stitches applied.
"While he's asleep, let's do the neutering," a voice said.

He heard it even though he was numb. His legs
no longer answered his call, and his whiskers
told him nothing, either. He heard them breathe
when they hovered over him.

Buster meowed once, and took a death.
Twice and thrice, he meowed again —
        he got the knack of this dying thing.
Still his heart beat. He twitched and meowed
      life *four*, life *five*, life *six*
        there they go
(are you sure you want to go through with this,
    Buster, no more mice ever?)
life *seven*, life *eight*,
    meow your lungs out to give up the *ninth*.

"We lost him, Doctor!" the assistant reported.
"He went into seizures and we lost him."

36.
The lady was furious
when they told her Buster was dead.
"I'm not paying for that operation,"
she shrieked, "since all you did
was kill my poor kitten."

"You can come get the body," they told her.

"What would I do with it?"

"We can cremate Buster.
You can have a nice little urn.
There's a pet cemetery in Queens."

"That sounds … suitable," the lady told them.

They told her what it would cost.

37.
Buster's remains went into a furnace.
Black smoke went up, a pile of ash
sank to the bottom,
all that remained of the noble cat.

A small bronze urn, engraved
with BUSTER and the single year
of his birth and departing,
was filled with the ashes.

No one ever came to claim it.

38.
The lady cried a great deal,
but then the winter came,
and she was busy at the office,
and there were the holidays,
and then a trip away,
and come spring

the only thing that bothered her
was that an owl kept coming
to her closed window, tap-
tapping on the glass and looking
at her. She had a dread
of owls and didn't know why
it kept tapping and peering,
tapping and peering.

After a while.
the owl stopped coming.

ABOUT THE POEMS

The works in this collection were all written or revised between Spring 2019 and Spring 2020. They are placed here pretty much in the order I completed the first drafts and posted them on my blog at brettrutherford.blogspot.com.

During the 12-month period, I was preparing a new edition of *The Pumpkined Heart*, not updated since 1973, intended to be a poetic memoir using three towns in Pennsylvania as their locale. This brought me to revise some poems not touched since the early 1970s. Some had been in *The Pumpkined Heart* in its 48-page chapbook form; some had been revised repeatedly in my later books; others had never been published anywhere.

The other new poems are all from my current home city of Pittsburgh, PA. A number are written out immediately upon awakening, from nights of vivid dreams. Many express the political and environmental anxieties around us as American society slides toward collapse under the rule of a sociopath. I have no assurance that the culture which I expected my poems to be part of, will endure.

A number of poems are adaptations or translations from poems in French, Chinese, Spanish Anglo-Saxon, Old English, Danish, and German. It is too late for me to become an emigré poet, but at least I walk in the shoes of poets around the globe, and across time. I have come to believe that translation of poems across cultures is essential and revitalizing. A poet of Ming Dynasty China, of Colombia in the 1890s, or of France in the 1820s, of a visionary German, Rilke, in 1911, reading a Latin funerary inscription in Venice — these are friends and peers, and if we but listen and trust our own voices, we speak together and to one another. I have no interest in literal translation. If I am re-speaking a line from the eleventh century, and a new line comes, it comes.

The following notes provide context for reading the poems.

THE INHUMAN WAVE was prompted by descriptions of the ferocity of Parisian women during the French Revolution, when they stormed Versailles and ripped Marie Antoinette's bedroom to shreds. and returned to Paris with heads on pikes, and the incendiary women of the Paris Commune many years later. It seems a fitting beginning to a collection of poems by a sworn neo-Romantic. The French Revolution is on our minds a lot these days.

PEELING THE ONION existed as a prose sketch in my book, *An Expectation of Presences*. As I prepared my big book of all my Pennsylvania poems for *The Pumpkined Heart* (2020), I recast it as a poem, finally. It is all true, and although it is, on the surface, about "things that happen to women," there may be more power and agency in Grandmother Butler than people suspect. There is more of her story to tell. The character of the evil stepfather is explored further in other poems in *The Pumpkined Heart*.

My journalism training included lessons in listening, to pick out individual conversations in a crowded room. I overhear the strangest things in diners. TALK AT THE DINER is a mix of real and imagined, a we careen backwards toward conformity and prejudice.

A year ago I was in Camden, NJ for New Year's and finally visited Walt Whitman's tomb. In THE HARVEST MOON IN CAMDEN, the good gray poet summons me there again at midnight for a chat about politics.

LET WINTER COME is ironic. It's a poem about not wanting to write another autumn poem, and about feeling old and finished, at age twenty-five! The revision enhances the irony somewhat.

TWO AUTUMN SONGS are lyrics of love found and lost. The second is inspired by the poetry of John Donne, and is an aria in the sense that it can, and should, be read in a single long breath. For a long time I have felt that "Come that downward plummet..." is the first poem that told me, definitively, what kind of poet I was to become.

THE PUMPKINED HEART reflects how much I hated New York City in the early days of my stay, and how I yearned for the beautiful landscape of Pennsylvania. This became the title poem of my second chapbook and was for many years my "homesick" poem.

AMONG THE PUT-AWAYS came from a dream, and may have been influenced by too much exposure to Arkham Asylum in Batman comics and the TV series *Gotham*. With a nod to zombies.

THE UNRELIABLE AUTUMN is written over an old sketch from my Edinboro college days. It has a snarky mood.

My poetry is littered with allusions to astronomy, nuclear physics, chemistry and biology — almost as frequent for me as calling upon some obscure Greek god. I have hesitated to footnote any of these, preferring to let them be little delights of discovery for those who get it. A poem like THE PERIODIC TABLE: HYDROGEN would take a science lesson to untangle so I just offer it and say, as Miss Jean Brodie did, "Well, for those who like that sort of thing, there's that sort of thing for them to like."

As we wake up each morning knowing that refugee Latin American children are being held in cages along our border, and that no popular uprising has occurred to stop it, I made a small protest in LETTERS ON A ROCK OUTCROP.

THE MILWAUKEE INTERVENTION was a skit or sketch in blank verse that I had proposed to write for Providence actress Wendy Feller, who starred in my plays on Jocasta and Empress Carlota of Mexico. Alas, she died before I ever put this to paper. It is a miniature character portrait of a tough-as-nails Mafia widow.

SQUANTO'S WIND. The John Hancock Building in Boston had to be surrounded with covered sidewalks for several years because window panes kept popping from their casements, hurtling to the pavement below. I imagined this as the doings of an enraged Manitou. My early version of the poem described only the window problem. It turns out the entire construction was jinxed, so now I have added more details. Once again, more facts make it possible to have a richer and better poem. Final note: the building is also the headquarters of Mitt Romney's firm, Bain Capital. Further 2019 touch-ups provoked me to include it in this collection.

SON OF DRACULA was originally a very short poem in the *Anniversarius* cycle of Autumn poems — a remembrance of a childhood fascination with Dracula, an adolescent nosebleed, and a brief October hospital stay in which I saw a graveyard on a nearby hillside, lit up by steel mill furnaces. A revision turned it into something more profound — a very specific memoir of adolescent angst in the coal-and-coke towns of Pennsylvania, and, at the end, my rebirth as a poet. This is also one of the first poems in which I tapped into my childhood for material. Recently I recast the poem as prose in an experiment, and then I found that some of the things I added to the prose belonged back in the poem. So here it is, yet again, maybe my most-revised poem.

While researching my ancestral home of Elsdon in Northumberland, I came across an account of a crime supernaturally punished, which I have told in AT THE ABBEY OF BURY ST. EDMUNDS. A medieval drawing of the attempted robbery adorns the poem.

THE MYSTERIES OF ELSDON CHURCHYARD reveals the town's presence during the Viking invasions, and as a part of Roman Britain.

RAVENS ARE WAITING, THE CROWS HAVE ARRIVED has as its initial impetus the arrival of thousands of crows who wintered in the oak trees of the University of Pittsburgh next to the Cathedral of Learning. After writing merely of the crows, and their uneasy relation with ravens, I then turned to a collection of Old English poetry and discovered a wonderful poem with gruesome details on the behavior of carrion crows, ravens, and hawks. This is my own version of that poem — happily I recall reading the entire *Anglo-Saxon Chronicle*, from which the poem is extracted, when I was a high-school student, so that was yet another return to old haunts. The third section of the poem takes the birds as omens of our present woes.

THE DEVELOPER is a wry adaptation of an 11th Century Anglo-Saxon poem.

ICELANDIC JUSTICE is adapted from the Old Norse.

MOVING TO PROVIDENCE, 1985, was sketched but never published. Now that I am a half-decade out of Rhode Island I can look back and realize it was actually as bad as this seeming satire makes it. What kept me there: New York drove me out, and Providence had cheap rent. I finally found friends there, mostly fellow exiles, and later enjoyed a decade of studying and working at the University of Rhode Island. But for the town, a shudder.

GERTRUDE AND THE REVENANT is from a Danish original. This Gothic poem is part of a group of things I am preparing for Volume Three of *Tales of Terror*, my anthology of supernatural poems. I am following Matthew Gregory Lewis's lead in adapting these poems in my own manner. I am seeking a sense of the Gothic and lyric, but without the use of rhyme.

Suetonius tells of a vicious practical joke played on some Roman senators and plutocrats by the cruel military Emperor Domitian. This monologue, DOMITIAN'S BLACK ROOM, attempts to capture the madness of Domitian, and his delight at terrifying his captives. As ever, Roman history has lessons for us.

Since Rome was on my mind, I awoke from a dream saying aloud the opening lines of I DREAMT I WAS THE APENNINES. It was written in one sweep. I added the Italian motto of the Abruzzi later, but otherwise this strange rhapsody is as it fell onto the page. I should like to hear it in Italian. I like to think that Leopardi would enjoy this poem.

I have written about THE OLD BRICK HOUSE AT CARPENTER-TOWN several times. This is the house in which I lived at ages four to seven, the house in which I was made to fear the arrival of the sinister Dr. Jones, a crazed World War I surgeon who amputated boys' arms and legs for sport.

THE WINNER considers the odds of winning the lottery.

THE TIMES THAT BURN THE BRAIN was in the 1973 chapbook, *The Pumpkined Heart*. A trifle, over-formal and obscure, it is a little better now.

I put A WING OF TIME on the shelf for a long time. It seemed self-indulgent, just a memoir of a time and place, even if it did have some happy language in it. I wanted the poem to succeed, but I wanted it to have a meaning. The poem suffered from narcissism, solipsism, even — the feeling that the poet is the center, watching people and places pass him by. In reality, I was the one passing. I haunted the place more than it haunted me. I am the meteor.

HITHER AND YON came from a 1973 fragment. Another trifle, THE DAEMON LEADS ME ON, existed in an almost inarticulate version in my 1973 book. It makes a little more sense in this version.

Edinboro Lake in Northwest Pennsylvania was uninhabited when John Culbertson settled there in 1796, arriving on trails newly cleared through the forest. Here, in 1796 EDINBORO LAKE, I have expanded my original from the 1970s, adding references to a mysterious entity that dwells in a bottomless swamp near the lake.

THE MIDNIGHT IBIS is one of two poems inspired by a watercolor given me by Providence artist Riva Leviten. The other was "Variations on the Ibis" in *Crackers at Midnight* (2017).

As I related in "Son of Dracula," listening to the *Fantastic Symphony* of Berlioz provoked one of my first attempts at poetry. To date, I have written poems interpreting or re-telling the program of the first and third movements of the symphony "Dreams, Passions," and "Scene in the Fields." Here I take on the fourth-movement MARCH TO THE SCAFFOLD, in which the hero of the Berlioz symphony goes to the Guillotine. I could not resist attempting the poem in French as well, as MARCHE AU SUPPLICE.

DANCE OF THE WITCHES' SABBATH. My earliest poem, happily destroyed, was an attempt to describe the fifth movement of the Berlioz *Fantastic Symphony,* in which the executed hero awakens in a cemetery, joined by demons and witches in a Round Dance. This spring I came upon Victor Hugo's French poem "Rond du Sabbat," whose details closely match the written program of the Berlioz symphony. Since Hugo's poem was published in 1825, apparently with great notoriety, and Berlioz wrote his symphony four years later, it is almost certain that this poem inspired the composer. Finding no English version of this poem since around 1900, I undertook this translation and adaptation. I have embellished a little, for, after all, this is my territory as much as Hugo's.

I witnessed the removal of a frozen corpse from a nearby house in Scottdale, after its occupant froze to death, told in THE COLD WAVE, 1958. For some time, I have envisioned a character whose last day I trace in this narrative poem, walking on streets I knew as a child. I also incorporated stories I had heard about the interactions of African-American and Hungarian coal miners.

In another time and I place, I was an old scholar in Ming Dynasty China. I know his name. I have his stone seal. I can sit in Autumn and see through his eyes. This Chinese painting, OLD SCHOLAR UNDER AUTUMN TREES, with a poem inscribed on it by the artist, comes from that world. I wrote this hastily in the middle of a Facebook posting years ago, and it only recently came to light. Shen Zhou (1427-1509) was a subversive painter resisting the court style of the Ming in favor of his own unique take on classics that had preceded his era. He collected Yuan paintings and was self-sufficient: he painted not for patrons, but for himself. He is a founder of the Wu School, and the painting I chose, with his own poem inscribed, shows his commitment to the idea of artist as scholar. How can I not admire Shen, my fellow outsider?

THE MAN WHO HATED TREES recalls a neighbor in Weehawken, NJ. As I later learned in Providence with Portuguese neighbors, some Mediterranean people dislike trees.

THE HEADLESS CROSS AT ELSDON returns again to the Rutherford ancestral home in Northumberland. A raven and a plucked eyeball feature in this gruesome ballad, which I have rendered, in my perverse manner, without rhyme.

THE THUNDERSTORM (ODE 2) was drafted when I was 21 years old, and was never published. I think I have finally unraveled this poem, depicting two very young men who are just as afraid of one another as they are attracted. It's part of my "obsession" cycle of poems in *The Pumpkined Heart*.

THE NIGHT I ALMOST FLEW is a recollection of levitation attempts near Edinboro Lake.

When Pittsburgh-area film-maker and photographer Tony Buba jokingly posted a photograph of a mattress found standing in a weed-lot, he asked friends to "explain" what his photo meant. This poem, A MATTRESS, VERTICAL, was my response.

THEY CLOSED HIS EYES is adapted and "written" over a classic Spanish poem. Gustavo Adolfo Bécquer (1836-1870), a Spanish poet from Seville, influenced by E.T.A Hoffmann and Heinrich Heine, wrote an elegiac poem titled "They Closed Her Eyes." I have gender-changed, "written over," and expanded upon his poem for this work, which is in memory of the 100,000 fatalities from HIV in New York during the 1980s, specifically those who wound up in the Potter's Field because no family would claim their bodies.

HE WAS NOT THERE, HE IS NOT HERE is an elegy for Brazilian-born dancer Kleber de Freitas, long-time companion of poet and publisher David Messineo. Kleber was videographer for many *Sensations Magazine* poetry events, and a beloved friend of our New Jersey poets' group. He had danced in a recreation of Nijinsky's choreography of *Afternoon of a Faun*, which is alluded to in the poem.

FROM THE LIPS OF THE LAST INCA is adapted from a poem by José Eusebio Caro (1817-1853), who lived in New Granada (present-day Colombia), and was co-founder of his nation's first literary journal, *La Estrella National,* in 1836. I have added salutations in Quechua, the language of the Incas, which were not in the original poem.

Regarding the volcano named Pichincha, which is in Ecuador, Wikipedia notes, "On May 24, 1822, General Sucre's southern campaign in the Spanish–American War of independence came to a climax when his forces defeated the Spanish colonial army on the southeast slopes of this volcano. The engagement, known as the Battle of Pichincha, secured the independence of the territories of present-day Ecuador."

NOCTURNE was written in 1892 by Colombian poet José Asuncion Silva, as "Nocturne III." He had lived in Europe and knew Mallarmé and other leading French poets. His poetry is a precursor of modernism in Latin American poetry, but in this one in particular, he inhabits the world and esthetics of Poe's poems. Suggestive of "Ulalume," hypnotic with its repetition and its shadowy images, this poem was also doubtless provoked by the death of Silva's beloved sister in the same year. Three years later, all the poet's unpublished works were lost in a shipwreck. A year after that, Silva committed suicide.

"Nocturne," written in free verse, defied the classical, formal mode of most poetry in Spanish.

In this adaptation I have made the supernatural suggestiveness of the poem stronger — it is not possible to work on a piece such as this without being completely overshadowed by "Ulalume." I have also introduced the concept of the double-shadow: the umbra is the dark, solid part of a shadow, and the penumbra is a shadow's vague, poorly-defined edges. Silva does not employ these terms, so this is my addition. I also removed the gender of the dead loved one, because, well, that it what I do. Silva repeats lines almost with a hypnotic intent, so I have done the same in my version, also permitting some exact phrases from the opening of the poem to find their way in again near the end, like a musical reprise.

It is simultaneously, a very Gothic poem, and a very modern poem. It is one of the most important Spanish-language poems I have engaged with.

In GUESTS AT OUR COUNTRY PLACE I combine satire with a chilling side-glance at rural law enforcement. As a country-dwelling friend cautioned, "Don't call the police unless you want someone shot."

THE SECRET was written as a missing, transitional poem for my Pennsylvania book, spanning the town where I was born (Scottdale) and the town where I went to high school (West Newton). It took me many decades to piece together the reasons why we "had to leave town."

THE F— POEM is a simple protest against the vulgarization of our English language. Some friends think I am silly, saying, "It is only a word," but I feel compelled to stand up for the language of Shakespeare and Shelley.

BEING TOO MUCH WITH THE STARS is an untitled poem by José Asunción Silva (1865-1896). It reminds me of H.P. Lovecraft's "Astrophobos," but even more of Walt Whitman's short poem about "The Learned Astronomers."

IN THE MIST came out of a recent dream. If I can imagine myself as the Apennine mountain range, being a lighthouse is an easy task.

MOONLIGHT IN THE CEMETERY is my adaptation of one of the most famous of all French Gothic-Romantic graveyard poems, Théophile Gautier's "Au Cimitière: Claire de Lune." The French original was set to music by Hector Berlioz.

THE OVERNIGHT ANGEL is from a notebook entry put down in the 1970s, about the same time I started working on my expansions of *The Duino Elegies*.

BECOMING INVISIBLE is based on a 1970s notebook sketch, and it portrays a well-known symptom of depression.

I was taken to a pow-wow many years ago, and met a young Iroquois who claimed to be able to pull airplanes down from the sky. WHAT THE SACHEM'S SON TOLD ME recreates his anger and rant accurately, but I am advised to say, "I did not see any falling planes."

NIAGARA AND BACK, 1966 recalls an actual hitch-hiking trip between Edinboro, PA and Niagara Falls, Canada, overshadowed by the Vietnam War. The United States drafted 382,010 men into military service that year, the highest total during the Vietnam War.

SUMMER OF 1967: CLEVELAND is a revision of a youthful poem that appeared in my earliest book, *Songs of the I and Thou*. As I rode from Pittsburgh to San Francisco on a Greyhound bus, I was reading Walt Whitman's "Song of the Open Road." Reading Whitman aloud in the Haight-Ashbury was my ticket of admission to the underground.

THINGS DONE IN CITIES is a reflection on the timelessness of city-building, and of corruption that grows in the shadows.

AFTER THE FUGUE IN B MINOR, written as an impressions of Bach's organ fugue, was left unpublished, a mere sketch. Recently I was able to figure out how to make more of its conceit, that of two amorous voices trapped in a fugue. All they needed was an invitation to a wild "Toccata," a show-off keyboard piece where the rules are relaxed, and frisky behavior between the clefs is tolerated.

THE AGONY OF ORCHIDS is based on a charming creature of my college days who drove young men to despair or attempted suicide, but, prompted by my recent reading of Lawrence Durrell, I got the idea of moving its locale to where a Venetian carnival could be used to dispose of rivals. (Durrell's novel, *Justine*, is set in Alexandria, Egypt, but includes a local version of the Venetian Carnival, replete with masks and black dominos.)

DEAD OF PROSE AT 29 is in memory of Stuart Milstein, the first Poet's Press author to die, and the youngest.

FATAL BIRDS OF THE SOUL

The work on these poems started in 1976, an attempt to translate, adapt, and expand upon the first two of Rainer Maria Rilke's *Duino Elegies*. The project was abandoned, the sketches only rediscovered in late 2019. In April 2020, I decided to complete the project, revising and expanding the original sketches and making them into a connected cycle of 21 poems.

This cycle is in no way an explication of Rilke, and the German poet would doubtless be horrified at the thought of a young atheist, neo-Romantic American poet of the 1970s making a palimpsest over his work, with the shades of Shelley, Walt Whitman, Poe, and even Lovecraft looking over his shoulder. That Rilke himself stepped away from the *Elegies* after writing the first two, only returning to the project some years later, gives some indication of the daunting power of Elegies 1 and 2. I, too, unsure of what I had done, and what was to be done with it, put the project aside.

Some of my recent work with translations and adaptations gave me the self-confidence to return to this perilous project, this time trusting my own voice and letting even more expansion emerge from the original material. If I have succeeded, Rilke's own words fit seamlessly into the flow of my own. I was in his thrall for a number of years, and his *Letters to a Young Poet* gave me comfort and inspiration when it was not coming from those around me. I already had a sense that in poems such as this, one is being "lived through" by language, creating a freestanding work that has its own existence, its own right to be.

To illustrate this cycle I turned to some of the Greek sculpture that makes clear some of Rilke's language about the vocabulary of touching in classic sculpture, and I was able to find a photo of the Latin tomb inscription Rilke found in Venice and copied down. These visual embellishments may help the reader recreate the visual elements of Rilke's musings on angels, on sculpture, and on Beauty in general.

The connecting subjects of The Poet, The Angel, and the Arrow are not from Rilke, who frequently uses "we" as his subject, subsuming the reader into his visions. I have detached this and made my poet a doubter, a skeptic, and one of Love's wounded. In this sense it is an interrogatory, whose only answer is that the Angel, despite all, *exists*.

I have no further explanation to offer. I could not paraphrase the "meaning" of this cycle if I tried. It passed through me on the way to the page. It will now have a life of its own.

BUSTER, or THE UNCLAIMED URN

This odd cycle of poems (or near-poems) came to be as a result of my editing of the papers of Barbara A. Holland (1925-1988). It is a posthumous collaboration/completion as explained in the following:

During her early years in the Greenwich Village poetry scene, Barbara A. Holland met two women poets with radically different outlooks and techniques. Ree Dragonette (1918-1979) and Emilie Glen (1906-1991) ran poetry salons and mentored and encouraged young poets. Both featured Barbara at their salons and introduced her to a wider circle of poets, editors, and publishers. Dragonette was a linguistic high-wire artist with a Maria Callas-like presence who had performed with jazz musicians, and I have always believed that Barbara perfected her style under Dragonette's shadow. Dragonette acknowledged this; Holland generally denied it.

Emilie Glen, who had a fifty-year stint as a full-time poet, knew the ropes of getting published in little magazines, and she almost certainly tutored Holland in how to compile lists of publishers, to submit queries, and to mail out poems on an almost industrial scale. Glen had published thousands of poems, and doubtless Holland wanted to achieve the same ubiquity. Glen was an avid bird-watcher and had a ready market for her poems about birds and the Central Park coterie of bird-watchers. She also loved cats, and placed hundreds of poems about real and imagined felines. Her forte was the urban short narrative poem, inhabiting the voice of a single character.

I find in Holland's notebooks a number of attempts to write about cats. They are tentative, almost phobic. She describes cats as creatures she attempts to approach and understand, but she never writes about a cat from the inside. She seldom succeeded in writing the kind of narrative poem from inside a character that was Glen's forte. Holland is an opera mad-scene singer, a Roderick Usher, a sensitive plant, a receiver of signals, all nerves. She can inhabit Medusa, a Sybil, Melusine, or Eurydice, but the story is already a given. She did not need to compete with either of her mentors/rivals, for she honed this style to perfection.

And yet ... in her notebooks I find her trying for an extended narrative, in sketches for, of all things, a cat book. *The Flying Cat* exists as sketches only, not in polished form. It has more than 30 sections, most with blank facing-pages, one section per page. At first glance, it appears to be an attempt at a children's book. The sketches are not yet poems, and they do not rhyme. Yet this is *not* a children's book: some of the details are gruesome, such as the description of unwanted kittens being drowned. The un-named woman who owns the flying cat is dreadful.

The Flying Cat makes perfect sense as an attempt to sketch a Gothic faux-children's book in the manner of her friend Edward Gorey, whose ghastly little illustrated books were a sensation in the 1960s and 1970s. Barbara and I were both avid Edward Gorey fans, and we talked about him many times. She may have had a mind to persuade Gorey to illustrate *The Flying Cat,* had she found a publisher. The difficulties were that, first, she did not write rhymed verse like Gorey's, whose text was full of Edwardian whimsy and camp humor; second, she let her plot trail off and never finished the story. She ends it abruptly after her Flying Cat leaves home, has several adventures, and then returns, to be taken to the veterinarian to look at why his wings have failed to grow as he matured from kitten to tom-cat. If it was to be a book in the Gorey vein, some calamitous ending was required.

Faced with this tantalizing fragment, I had two choices. I could leave it for future scholars to pore over in the Holland papers, or I could attempt to edit and complete the work in the Gorey vein. I have done the latter. In a poet's frenzy, I edited, "overwrote," and added to Holland's original. The story is complete, and Buster, the flying cat, comes to his terrible end. In the Gorey manner, I changed the title to "Buster, or The Unclaimed Urn," and made Barbara Holland's name into an anagram, "Abadon Barr-Hall." This has been a light-hearted diversion in the midst of the somber enterprise of publishing Holland's notebooks and papers. It is not the best of Holland, and it is not the best of me, since I did not feel empowered to do more than a *pentimento* over her original, and then completing the far edge of the canvas. I hope it gives pleasure.

ABOUT THE POET

Brett Rutherford, born in Scottdale, Pennsylvania, began writing poetry seriously during a stay in San Francisco. During his college years at Edinboro State College in Pennsylvania, he published an underground newspaper and printed his first hand-made poetry chapbook. He moved to New York City, where he founded The Poet's Press in 1971. For more than twenty years, he worked as an editor, journalist, printer, and consultant to publishers and nonprofit organizations.

After a literary pilgrimage to Providence, Rhode Island, on the track of H.P. Lovecraft and Edgar Allan Poe, he moved there with his press. *Poems From Providence* was the fruit of his first three years in the city (1985-1988), published in 1991. Since then, he has written a study of Edgar Allan Poe and Providence poet Sarah Helen Whitman (briefly Poe's fiancée), a biographical play about Lovecraft, and his second novel, *The Lost Children* (Zebra Books, 1988). His poetry, in volumes both thematic and chronological, can be found in *The Pumpkined Heart* (1973, 2020), *Poems From Providence* (1991, 2011), *Things Seen in Graveyards* (2007), *Anniversarius: The Book of Autumn* (1984-2020), *Twilight of the Dictators* (1992, 2009), *The Gods As They Are, On their Planets* (2005, 2012), *Whippoorwill Road: The Supernatural Poems* (1998, 2005, 2012, 2020), *An Expectation of Presences* (2012), *Trilobite Love Song* (2014), *Crackers at Midnight* (2018), and *The Doll Without A Face* (2019).

Returning to school for a master's degree in English, Rutherford completed this project in 2007, and worked for University of Rhode Island in distance learning, and taught for the Gender and Women's Studies Department. There, he created courses on "The Diva," "Women in Science Fiction," and "Radical American Women."

He has prepared annotated editions of Matthew Gregory Lewis's *Tales of Wonder*, the poetry of Charles Hamilton Sorley, A.T. Fitzroy's antiwar novel *Despised and Rejected*, the collected writings of Emilie Glen and Barbara A. Holland, and selected fiction by Mikhail Artsybashev and Leonid Andreyev (*Two Russian Exiles*, 2019).

ART CREDITS

Cover: *The Temptation of St. Anthony.* Matthias Grünewald.

End leaves: Greek funerary stele. Metropolitan Museum, New York City.

Page 59: Medieval illumination drawing depicting the attempted robbery of the Abbey at Bury St. Edmunds.

Pages 63 to 67: Churchyard of St. Cuthbert's Church, Elsdon, Northumberland, England.

Page 91: Ruins of brick house at Carpentertown, near Hecla, PA. Photo by the author.

Page 103. Maples trees at Edinboro Lake, Edinboro, PA. Photo by the author.

Facing page 106: *The Ibis.* Watercolor by Riva Leviten. Collection of the author.

Page 128: Painting and poem by Shen Zhou, 1470 CD.

Facing Page 137: Photograph by Tony Buba. With permission by the photographer.

Facing page 190: Detail of Greek funerary stele. Metropolitan Museum, New York City.

Page 195: Digital art from detail of *Archangel Michael Tramples Satan.* Guido Reni (1575-1642). Oil on canvas. Santa Maria della Concezione, Rome.

Facing Page 206: Tomb inscription of Helmanus Gulielmus at Santa Maria Formosa, Venice. Photo from Wikimedia Commons by "Jodo50931," 2007.

Facing Page 225: Greek funerary stele. Metropolitan Museum, New York City.

Page 227: Another Greek funerary stele. Location unknown.

ABOUT THIS BOOK

The body text for this book is Cheltenham, a typeface designed in 1896 by architect Bertram Goodhue and printer Ingalis Kimball. The fully-developed typeface was designed by Morris Fuller Benton at American Typefounders and released in hot metal in 1902. Until the 1930s it was a dominant type for headlines, and its legibility and character made it a popular face in Arts and Crafts publications, including those of The Roycrofters. It is still employed for headlines by *The New York Times.* The digital version employed in this book is ITC Cheltenham, designed in 1975 by Tony Stan for International Typeface Corporation. The small titles are set in Cheltenham Ultra. The title-page and cover are a mix of Franklin Gothic, a favorite display face from the hot metal era, and Cheltenham.

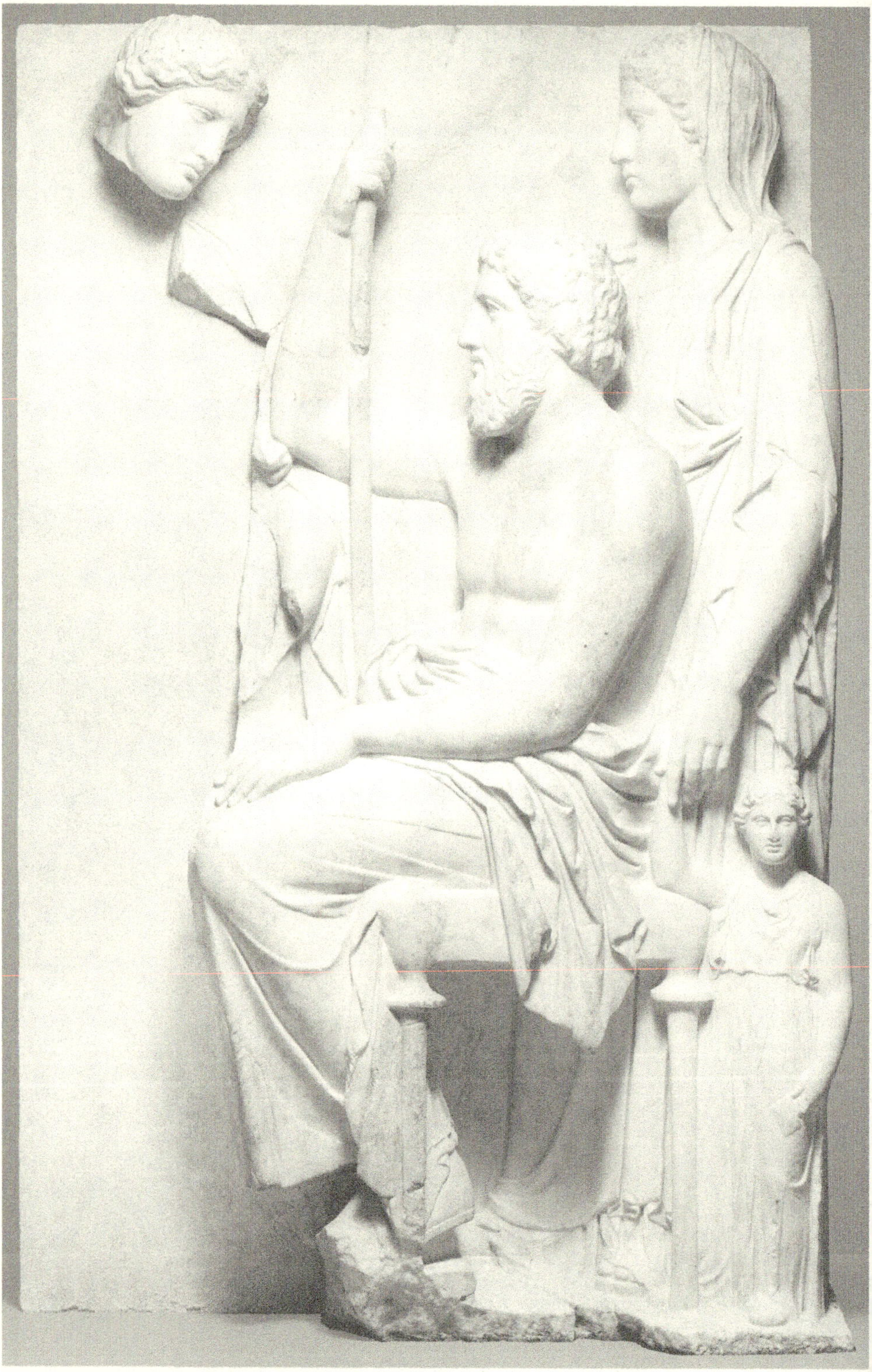

Made in the USA
Monee, IL
14 April 2021